The Successful Divorce

What You Must Know and Do Now

By John M. Wood
Attorney at Law

Published by
Professional Solutions Group
Books Division
Dallas, Texas

A softcover original

Published by

Books Division
203 Lake Ridge Village, Suite 405
Dallas, Texas 75238
1-800-465-1508

THE SUCCESSFUL DIVORCE: What You Must Know And Do Now
Alabama Edition

ISBN 0-9659273-0-X

Library of Congress Catalogue Card Number 97-68854

Printed in the United States of America

10 9 8 7 6 5 4 3 2 1

To God, for giving me the talent and the skills to help other people;

To my lovely wife, for helping me apply that talent to make my dreams come true;

To my mother, for the wonderful team we made after my parents' divorce; and

To my clients, for giving me the opportunity to make a difference in their lives.

NOTICE

State laws and legal precedents vary greatly and change over time. Because of this, the reader should not use this book for specific legal advice. Every divorce case and post-divorce action is unique, requiring the advice of those versed in the laws of the jurisdiction where the action is taken. It must be understood, therefore, that this book will provide readers only with a general overview of the divorce process and divorce and post-divorce issues, so that they may take legal action or otherwise address these issues somewhat better informed. This book is not intended to provide legal advice and you should consult an attorney for specific information related to your personal situation.

The people described in this book are not meant to represent anyone living or deceased. No real names or precise fact patterns have been used, to protect the privacy of the parties involved.

Any similarities between actual people or situations and the characters described in this book are purely coincidental.

TABLE OF CONTENTS

PART ONE
Pretrial: Readying Yourself For the Battle

PART THREE
What Happens After the Divorce

ACKNOWLEDGMENTS

Success — to laugh often and much; to win the respect of intelligent people and the affection of children; to know even one life has breathed easier because you have lived .... This is to have succeeded.
                                    Ralph Waldo Emerson

Having endured my parents' divorce as a child, I feel uniquely qualified to describe the pain of divorce and the struggle to overcome it. My parents' divorce has given me a tremendous insight into my priorities in life. My mother and I formed a never-ending bond while overcoming the obstacles inherent in an ugly divorce. I am thankful for having a wonderful mother, sister and brother. We are close today, in part, because of the struggles of the past. And it is the confidence and security they gave me that allows me to write a book with the curious title, THE SUCCESSFUL DIVORCE.

I believe that my intense focus on the family today is a direct result of the experiences I encountered as a young child. If anything positive came out of that terrible situation, it is the understanding of my primary goal. In practicing divorce and custody law, I want to help my clients successfully maneuver through the problems and situations that other people have been forced to endure alone.

I have been blessed with a wonderful family. Today, my wife and I have two lovely daughters who are the major focus of our lives. I also have a successful law practice, where I get to spend each day helping others. I thank my wife for encouraging me to follow my dreams and take the steps necessary to reach my goals.

Perhaps the greatest example of my wife's confidence in me is the enthusiasm she exhibited when I told her I wanted to leave my job with one of the state's largest firms to practice matrimonial law. She simply asked me if I thought I could do it. When I told her that I could, she said, "Let's go for it."

This book would not have been possible without the support

of my wife, family and close friends. I would like to thank my wife for taking a chance on a new law practice with a few clients and a lot of hopes and dreams. There is no real way to thank all of the wonderful friends, attorneys and clients who have all helped make this book a reality.

This has been a two-year process. From the bottom of my heart, I thank all of my clients for allowing me the opportunity to help them, and now you. I hope this book will help some of you avoid the heartache I have witnessed others endure.

— John M. Wood

ABOUT THE AUTHOR

John M. Wood has a law practice in Birmingham, Alabama devoted almost exclusively to matrimonial law, including child custody and divorce litigation. He left a successful tenure with one of the state's largest firms because of a desire to develop a practice concentrating in divorce and custody issues.

Recently, John formed Wood & Shaw, L.L.C., with his close friend, Paul B. Shaw, Jr. Paul concentrates in civil and business litigation, and the firm represents several Birmingham-based and Fortune 500 companies. Paul's expertise is useful to nearly every divorce client the firm serves.

As a child of divorce himself, John Wood is keenly aware that domestic problems often present clients with the most important legal issues they will ever face.

His goal in writing THE SUCCESSFUL DIVORCE, and in the practice of law, is to educate clients that decisions related to divorce must be thoroughly thought out, because they will have long-lasting consequences. The effect of divorce lasts throughout the lifetimes of the parties, including not only the husband and wife, but the children and other family members as well.

As a result, decisions made during the divorce will impact the entire family and create a host of new situations and challenges for everyone. To reach a successful conclusion in every case, John has the goal of providing the highest quality legal representation while educating each client about the steps involved in the legal process, and keeping the client informed about every step taken in the case.

John is married and the father of two girls. He is an active member of Dawson Memorial Baptist Church and supports numerous charitable organizations, including The Big Oak Ranch home for children.

John graduated from the prestigious Georgetown University Law School and is a member of the American Bar Association, Alabama Bar Association and the Birmingham Bar Association. He serves as Treasurer of the Executive Committee of the Family Law Section of the Alabama State Bar Association and on the Fee Arbitration Committee of the Birmingham Bar Association.

Recently, John was honored by the BIRMINGHAM BUSINESS JOURNAL as one of the city's *Top 40 Under 40*, recognizing young leaders in the business and civic arena.

— The Publisher

PREFACE

I will consider my earthly existence to have been wasted unless I can recall a loving family, a consistent investment in the lives of people and an earnest attempt to serve the God who made me.

Dr. James Dobson

How I went from Georgetown Law School and one of the largest law firms in the state to practicing matrimonial law is a remarkable story that I am proud to share. I truly believe that I received a blessing from God in being given the opportunity to help people in this area of the law. This is perhaps best illustrated by the following story. At my previous law firm, I was traveling out of town 20 to 25 days per month and was miserable because of the strain it put on my marriage. I had received several job offers from other firms for substantially more money. However, I did not want to continue in another firm of more than 150 attorneys. I felt God wanted me to work in another way. I had always been fascinated by custody issues as long as I can remember, so I began to develop a plan that would allow me to move in that direction. For nearly a year, I went to the courthouse to study divorce and custody trials and what the clients and attorneys did right and wrong.

One night while I was on an interview with another large firm, my wife attended a bible study class. She asked everyone to keep me in their thoughts. At the time, I was struggling with whether to take the lucrative job offer or start a practice concentrating in matrimonial law. Obviously, we had financial concerns. How could we afford this wonderful idea and how we could make it? Immediately, a woman she did not know stood up and asked her if she was serious. This woman, a lawyer, was having her third child and was trying to find someone to take over her law practice. My wife immediately called me to tell me this unbelievable answer to our prayers. Twelve days later I was in my new office, and the rest is history. Since then,

I have been blessed with a wonderful practice, a fantastic law partner, a strong client base, a great team of professionals in my office who help me do my job and many dear friends in the legal community.

As a result, I can truly say that through God all things are possible. All of this happened because this area of the law involves one of the most important issues that most individuals will ever encounter during their lifetime. Throughout my practice, I have tried to guide my clients to understand that there are implications for each and every decision they make related to their divorce.

In my opinion, educating the client helps that person to understand the consequences of his or her actions and hopefully can prevent a bad situation from becoming a disastrous situation. This is why I appreciate so much the opening quote by James Dobson. If you remember anything from reading this book, please remember that every step you take in your custody or divorce case will have far-reaching implications throughout not only your lifetime, but the lives of your children, family members and friends. For that reason alone, please proceed cautiously and wisely.

— John M. Wood

INTRODUCTION

Divorce is a twentieth century phenomenon. Since World War II, when women were forced to work in the factories and discovered they could care for themselves, the number of divorces has steadily grown. With the adoption of so-called "no-fault" divorce statures by many states in the 1960's and 70's, divorce became easier and more accepted.

THE SUCCESSFUL DIVORCE is more than a book title. It describes an intelligent approach to the process. Each divorce is unique, and the various facts, assets, debts and faults of each individual marriage will be considered in the resolution of the divorce. Anyone who blindly enters into the divorce arena must understand that the consequences of your actions will follow you throughout your life. But divorce doesn't have to be the end of your life. On the contrary, THE SUCCESSFUL DIVORCE is one that you move into with knowledge and foresight, protecting yourself and the ones you love. At the end of the process, you have not "lost your shirt," but instead you have your life back and your children are intact.

The entire process of divorce oftentimes is referred to as "jungle warfare." For each spouse, the pathway is dark and unfamiliar territory, much like a jungle. Further, the process itself often feels like warfare, where each side plans skirmishes and court battles before the ultimate resolution of the case.

Many people today say that government should make divorce more difficult to obtain. Several states are attempting to repeal the statutes that make divorce easy, while others are trying to make it more difficult to get married in the first place. But until we see the curve on the graph of divorce turn downward, the battle lines are drawn.

This book makes numerous references to the husband and the wife, as well as referencing "she" and "he," the "parents" and the "parties." It should be apparent from the context that I am talking about the people who are divorcing. This material is intended to be applicable to both the husband and the wife. For purposes of this book, please accept the "he/she" references as being applicable to both parties and not any kind of gender-based designation, including references to "the attorney." There are many excellent male and female matrimonial lawyers, and all references are intended to be applicable to both.

The examples used in this book are loosely based on prior cases. Most examples are composites of people and situations I have become familiar with in the Alabama court system. No references should be construed to indicate that only a wife or only a husband could act in a particular manner. Plenty of husbands and wives act equally horribly, both during the marriage and pending divorce. In fact, one of the most critical questions I can ask during an initial interview is, "Now that you have told me how terrible your spouse can be, what is he (or she) going to say about you?" If that spouse says, "Oh, I haven't ever done anything," I must then determine what secrets are out there that make my client look bad, and what my client has failed to tell me. If the omissions are serious, I have to determine if I can represent a person who is not totally honest with me.

In most marriages, there is plenty of fault to go around. Women have affairs and men have affairs, women take drugs and men take drugs, women lie and men lie. In fact, one well-known domestic judge once said after a heated trial that since the parties told such different stories and both parties had sworn under oath that they were telling the truth, it was clear that they could not have been married to each other. The amazing fact in many cases is that each party will claim the other side is lying. You need to realize that your spouse may lie to ensure a favorable result. If this type of behavior is expected, get ready for it, so it won't disrupt your case.

This book is primarily based on the present statutes and currently controlling case law for the state of Alabama, since that is where I practice. However, if you reside in a state other than Alabama, the key concepts in this material are still worth reading to familiarize you with the divorce process. For example, you will need to hire an attorney and prepare for trial, no matter where you reside. I have attempted to make this material serve as a guide to preparing for your divorce, regardless of where you live. But this is not a how-to book. You cannot simply read this book and feel that you are prepared to represent yourself in a divorce. There are times when people can represent themselves. We talk about those times later, in a chapter on uncontested divorces. If your divorce is truly uncontested, you may not need an attorney. However, I strongly recommend that you seek counsel. Usually the divorce process is too complicated even for the attorney who is not a matrimonial specialist, let alone non-lawyers.

Because the legal situations cited here are, for the most part, based on Alabama law, you will need to consult an attorney in your state to determine the specific applicability of any particular provisions.

THE SUCCESSFUL DIVORCE addresses the divorce process and its various stages, from the selection of an attorney through settlement or trial, to the difficulty of enforcing your divorce decree, to post-divorce actions. Along the way, issues ranging from custody to property division are discussed. Remember, however, that this material merely serves as an overview of the major issues surrounding a divorce, and each case hinges on its own facts. This book should not be used as a replacement for specific legal advice or independent counsel.

— John M. Wood

PART ONE

Pretrial:
Readying Yourself For the Battle

Don't go to divorce court for justice.
Go simply for a conclusion.

Anonymous divorce lawyer

CHAPTER 1

In a Perfect World,
I Would Be Out of a Job

We live in the era of disposable relationships. Everywhere we look, people are shedding themselves of their mates. Over the past decade, about one half of all marriages have ended. Someone once said that we treat our spouses like we do our socks, discarding them after light use. Only we're really much nicer to the socks, since we don't actually throw them out.

There's Too Much Divorce

The toll of all this divorce on our families has been devastating. Adults become alienated, and some children never fully recover. The ripple effect of divorce on the social fabric of our entire society is felt by many. It is seen in problems relating to our schools, the incidence of crime, teenage pregnancy and other undesirable situations.

Because of the detrimental effects of divorce, I would not encourage anyone to consider divorce unless no other options exist. Anyone contemplating such a move should make use of every resource — marital or individual therapy, substance abuse counseling, the words of a pastor, or the guidance of a close friend or advisor —

to avoid the breakup of the marriage. In a perfect world, resources like these would keep more marriages together — and I would practice in another area of the law. But this isn't a perfect world, and many marriages cannot be saved. If all efforts to save the marriage have been exhausted and a divorce is inevitable, all you can do is make sure you have a "successful" divorce, one that is handled with diligence and care.

Myth of the "Kind" Spouse

When divorce becomes inevitable, an alarming number of people believe a spouse will be kind. But you can be taken advantage of and can lose custody of your children, as well as some or most of your most valuable assets, to a "kind" spouse. For this reason, you must recognize that what happens to you in a divorce depends upon the actions you take to protect yourself.

Initially, you may refuse to believe your divorce could possibly become contested, or that the person you shared your life with would refuse to do "what's right." You may be in for a terrible shock when the former bread winner refuses to pay child support or fights for custody of the children. You may refuse to believe your kind and loving soon-to-be ex could possibly be having an affair. The shock can turn to rage when you discover this information after you've executed a settlement agreement on terms favorable to that spouse.

As a divorce attorney, I deal with a lot of family heartache. When I work to reach a settlement, my ultimate goal is to resolve the divorce with the least amount of disruption possible, especially if young children are involved. However, both parties must be willing to reach a settlement. If one party is willing to settle the case, and the other party refuses to accept the fact that a spouse is entitled to a fair distribution of the assets under the divorce, a settlement is unlikely. At that point, you may be entering into a war zone and have to ready yourself for battle.

I remember one man who refused to accept that his wife of more than 20 years was entitled even to her clothes, since in his opinion they were in "his house." Never mind that they had paid for the house together and the wife's name was on the deed. In cases like this, settlement is often impossible. This kind of inflexible attitude hurts both parties. The woman was dismayed that she had to fight so hard for what rightfully should have been hers. No matter how much punishment he inflicted on his longtime mate, in the end he was convinced that she had gotten too much.

Difficult Beginning, Difficult End

If your spouse is difficult during the divorce, this behavior doesn't end when the judge drops his gavel. Many cases result in post-divorce litigation, either dealing with the custody of children or the handling of property that, for whatever reason, remains in the names of both parties. Changes in the access of parents to their children can be especially sticky, and one party may decide not to cooperate in the renovation or sale of property merely to anger the other.

If you are contemplating a divorce, are already in the middle of one, or would like to make changes to a divorce that's already granted, recognize the disaster you may be creating. You need to get sound advice on every decision you make from an expert, not from your mother, a friend or Oprah. For purposes of this action alone, your spouse is now the enemy. You are right at the edge of a battlefield called the legal system, about to go to war. If the war starts, you need to be ready, knowledgeable about the rules of war, and prepared to face the consequences of battle.

*May your last decision as a married couple
be your best decision as a married couple.*

An Alabama Circuit Court Judge

CHAPTER 2

Can An Awful Divorce Make Up
For A Bad Marriage?

We should approach divorce the way we did as a child, when a bully punched us in the stomach. Both are devastating. They take your breath away. And as much as it hurt, raging headlong after the bully usually got you hurt even worse. It made more sense to sit down, catch your breath and consider your response.

Before proceeding with a divorce action, you should exhaust every avenue available to save the marriage. Seek help from your church, marriage counselors and support groups. Talk with co-workers, family members and friends. If you have children, talk to people who've done exactly what you are now contemplating. See how it affected their children and themselves. Gather information, but don't reveal too much of yourself. Any one of these people could be called to testify against you at trial.

"In my experience, many people jump into the idea of divorce as a way of trying to find relief for their emotional pain," says Bart Grooms, M.Div., M.Ed., of the Samaritan Counseling Center of Baptist Health System in Birmingham. "I try to show couples that most people can find healing for their pain by making changes in the relationship, and that they and their children stand to gain enormously.

"Divorce will always be an option for people who simply cannot improve things no matter how hard they work at it. But that should be a last resort. It's amazing how many people stop thinking about divorce once they realize that constructive change is possible."

Divorce Won't Cure All Marriage Problems

A divorce is not a short-term fix for marital problems. It is an emotionally draining process which, in fact, may create more problems after the marriage than were encountered during the marriage. A good attorney should make every effort to ensure that you are prepared for the process and are aware of opportunities to save your marriage.

At the same time, however, you may be caught in the middle of an abusive or violent situation that may escalate into tragedy. In an abusive or controlling situation, a decision must be made immediately, for your safety and the safety of your children. Once that decision has been made, you must get sound legal advice and utilize the police and court system to prevent further abuse.

Realize that even though you are divorcing, you may still have considerable contact with your former spouse. If there are no children involved, you may never have to deal with your spouse after the divorce. If you do have children, usually you will communicate regularly with your former spouse concerning the care of the children. Both parents have legal rights related to the children, and are normally afforded certain protections by the court. Therefore, consider what the relationship will be like between the parties after the divorce.

You may be surprised how difficult it is to raise children in two separate homes. Daily responsibilities are greatly magnified with only one person doing them. You may have total responsibility for thousands of lunches, carpools and practice sessions or sporting events. You may have to make last-minute decisions when you have a sick child and you have to go to work. And you may constantly worry about the lack of good parental influences. Even in marriages where one parent is the primary caretaker for the children, the other spouse usually serves as a backup caretaker in an emergency. At the same time, you may be amazed how peaceful life can be without a difficult spouse. This is part of THE SUCCESSFUL DIVORCE. I am always thrilled to see how clients rediscover themselves after they get away from a controlling or abusive spouse. The decision to divorce must be made on an individual basis, but it can only be made after assessing all the present and future issues.

Getting Advice From Oprah and Others

"I just saw a show on Oprah about custody and she said I need to...," said a former client. Many clients begin their research into their rights this way. A long line of co-workers, friends and family members will offer you plenty of advice if you decide to divorce. Talk shows will lure you with topics like "Leaving your Husband" or "The Mistakes You Can Make in Your Divorce." Magazine articles on failing relationships and the divorce process will call out to you from newsstands. But not one of these sources knows all the secrets of *your* marriage, and no one can give you accurate advice without all of the facts. This information is based on a limited experience with situations that are distinctly different from yours. You will hear that women always get more than 50 percent of the assets, and that fathers never get custody of the kids. As a result, these "war stories" can skew your idea of what is possible. Inevitably, they will damage your pursuit of THE SUCCESSFUL DIVORCE.

The time to seek help from family and friends is before you decide the divorce is inevitable. After the decision is made, lean on family and friends for emotional support, but turn to an expert for legal advice. Many people are reluctant to ask for advice about marital problems because they are embarrassed or ashamed. But a lack of knowledge of issues related to divorce can result in grossly misguided decisions.

Hire As Much Expertise in Family Law As You Can Afford

People should pay at least as much to get divorced as they do to get married. An amazing number of people fail to get legal advice until after they feel they were "cheated" in their divorce. People who don't have a problem paying whatever it costs for an expert to repair a car will "save money" by turning to mother, brother, sister, a friend or even Oprah for a legal opinion when it comes to divorce. Often people will consult an attorney who is a friend or an acquaintance, but who has little or no expertise in divorce law. Granted, some situations are simple enough to be handled by a legal generalist. But when you are gambling with your children's lives and your financial future, you are rolling the dice, potentially making the wrong decision to venture through the mine field with novice help. This is not a gamble you should be willing to take.

If you are unhappy with the outcome of your divorce, the court will not accept the excuse that you did not think your spouse would be unfair. If you had an opportunity to obtain expert legal advice, and chose not to because you did not know any better or did not want to pay for it, the court is not likely to change the agreement you foolishly signed. If you do not properly handle your divorce action the first time, the adage that "you made your bed, so lie in it" will become hauntingly true in a post-divorce action.

Post-Divorce Actions Are Expensive

Even if you are able to amend a problem by filing a post-divorce action, often you spend several times more to modify a decree after a divorce than the original problem would have cost. I cannot

10

even begin to describe the emotion that clients display when told they gave up custody of children in the divorce and may not be able to change custody now.

One young woman came to our office soon after her divorce was final. She had wanted custody of her little girl, but mistakenly gave her husband custody in the divorce agreement. The husband told the wife that he did not want custody, but that the papers had to say he got custody for the judge to approve the agreement "because the wife had not been in her apartment long enough." The wife was not represented by counsel and signed the divorce agreement, genuinely believing that she was going to get custody in spite of what the agreement specified, because "her husband had told her she would."

Within days after executing the agreement, the wife found out that the husband had been having an affair and that he was not going to allow her to keep the child because "the papers said that he got custody." Needless to say, the wife had to incur a tremendous financial and emotional expense to ultimately get her child back.

We were able to reverse the outcome of that case, but most of the time people create an unfixable mess because they did not hire an expert in the beginning. There is a plumbing company in Birmingham that uses the slogan, "We Repair What Your Husband Fixed." This could easily be adapted for many divorce lawyers into "We Fix What You Messed Up." Yet, in dealing with much more serious matters of custody, many parents are forced to accept the fact that they have lost their children due to their own bad decisions.

It's difficult to tell which gives some couples the most happiness, the minister who marries them, or the judge who divorces them.

Mary Wilson Little, from "I Do to I'll Sue"

CHAPTER 3

An Uncontested Divorce: Is There Any Such Thing

A truly uncontested divorce exists only in the rarest of circumstances. This kind of divorce usually involves two people — who can no longer agree on anything — agreeing on every issue related to the dissolution of their marriage.

If one spouse does exactly what the other spouse wants, an uncontested divorce will happen every time. But when you combine the parties' egos, pride, jealousy, rage, and resentment, with the resolution of custody and property issues, it is unlikely that both can forge an agreement. We talk to people every day who want to know the fee for an uncontested divorce, because the divorcing parties have an agreement and "all they need is for a lawyer to prepare the papers."

When we ask whether the other party agrees with the terms of the divorce, the usual response is "No, but what do I care about that? This is what I want." A situation like this usually will become contested. Even when the client says the other spouse is in total agreement, we rarely believe it until the documents are signed and filed with the court.

Restraining Yourself

Many agreements that would have worked out fall apart because one spouse got in a horrible fight with the other before the papers were executed. For that reason alone, clients should keep their mouths shut until the divorce is final. Emotions run high during the resolution of a divorce. One party may say something horrible to the other spouse and a simple uncontested divorce becomes contested out of nothing more than pride and anger.

In an uncontested divorce, it is possible, although not recommended, for the parties to use only one attorney. However, that attorney can legally represent only one party in the divorce and cannot advise the other party of the legal consequences of any decisions made. The attorney is looking out for the best interests of only one client, and the other party's rights could be grossly affected by the terms of the agreement. In this rare occasion, just make sure you are the spouse with the attorney. Otherwise, prepare yourself for a potential disaster that can affect you the rest of your life.

Filing the Documents

In a real sense, all divorces begin as contested divorces. Think about it. If there was not some kind of disagreement, the parties would not be getting a divorce. In some cases, though, all of the issues are resolved early. An "uncontested divorce" can be obtained by a lawyer drafting the necessary pleadings and documents required to be filed with the court. Under this scenario, the party filing for divorce is called the plaintiff, and the opposing party is called the defendant on all of the court pleadings. The lawyer will file all of the executed documents with the court and the parties may be able to avoid appearing in court. These documents include the following:

Complaint: This is the first document filed in a divorce. It contains certain factual information related to the parties involved, as well as the grounds for the divorce. Generally an uncontested divorce is obtained on the basis of incompatibility, that the parties have different interests and have grown apart, and that such incompatibility is irremediable and irreconcilable.

Answer and Waiver: This document, which is typically the second one filed, is executed by the opposing party and answers the specific allegations contained in the complaint. It also waives any other notice requirements so the divorce can be filed and the process completed without additional delays.

Acknowledgment of Representation: This document is executed by the opposing party and states that he or she is aware that the attorney involved represents the other party, and that he or she has had an opportunity to consult with or obtain other counsel.

Testimony: This document is executed by the plaintiff, and consists of a sworn statement of the grounds for the divorce, so that the parties are not required to be present in court prior to the divorce being granted.

Settlement Agreement: The most critical document of the divorce, the settlement agreement specifies the agreement reached between the parties. Anything not specified or addressed in this document will not likely be binding on the parties and could result in conflict in the future.

Final Judgment of Divorce: Executed by the trial court judge, this document grants the divorce, approves the settlement agreement and makes it binding on both parties.

Once all documents have been executed by the parties, they are filed with the court and the judge will execute the Final Judgment of Divorce. In 1997, the Alabama legislature began to require a 30-day waiting period after the complaint is filed before a divorce can be granted. The purported goal is to ensure that parties have not proceeded too quickly in obtaining the divorce, and to provide an additional opportunity for reconciliation.

On the other hand, this 30-day period also can result in an attempted repudiation of the agreement and the divorce becoming contested. Sometimes the parties have a disagreement during the waiting period. Of course, once an agreement is filed with the court, it is extremely difficult, if not impossible, to change it without filing a separate action to modify the decree.

If all the documents have been prepared properly, the parties are not usually required to appear in court and the judge will sign the divorce decree within several days or weeks.

Every divorce sinks to the level of the most irrational party.

Melvin Belli

CHAPTER 4

The Contested Divorce:
When Two Reasonable People Can't
Agree on Anything

A contested divorce is any divorce in which the parties cannot agree on the terms of the settlement. It can involve the parties and their lawyers attempting to negotiate an out-of-court settlement, or it can involve a full-blown litigated divorce in which a lawsuit is filed and tried in a courtroom.

If a divorce is being negotiated, the attorneys generally attempt to resolve the matter without a trial. Usually, though, a lawsuit is filed by one of the parties, and discovery and settlement negotiations are conducted while the parties await a trial date.

Your Spouse Is Now The Enemy

To get ready for a contested divorce, remember that your spouse is no longer your friend. At least for the time being, he or she has become the enemy. This person is often either trying to take your children or prevent you from receiving some material asset you believe you deserve. One of the biggest mistakes you can make in a divorce is thinking your spouse will give you what you want. Gener-

19

ally, when this mistake occurs, the opposing spouse is only nice as he or she leaves the courtroom with the children or all the marital assets.

This does not mean that a divorce has to be ugly from the beginning. But a sense of realism at this time of your life is essential to THE SUCCESSFUL DIVORCE. Friends, family and former love interests may say bad things about you, hurtful things said in bitterness. These things may not be true. Or what they say may be factual, but there is a good reason for your behavior. No one else may understand why you want out of a marriage, or why you wish to fight so hard to stay with a person who treats you so badly. All of this is part of the alienation and distrust inherent in the divorce process, and you should be prepared for that.

Your Divorce Strategy

From a strategic view, all contested divorces should be handled as though they were going to trial. If settlement efforts are successful, you are miles ahead of the game. If settlement efforts fail, you are not left unprepared. Fair settlements happen when you obtain adequate information at the start of your case. However, you might not even know all of the marital assets and may be relying on what your spouse has said should be the asset division. If your spouse has not disclosed all of the assets or is keeping other secrets, you may be entering into the settlement agreement uninformed.

Since you have the opportunity to determine all of the marital assets or other factors present, the court usually will not change the agreement after the divorce has been granted, just because you didn't discover all the assets when you had the opportunity.

A few years ago, a dear friend of mine gave her husband custody of their child out of fear that the divorce would become contested and the child would have to go through a bitter divorce. She did not hire a lawyer because she thought the husband would "play fair." But the husband had been abusive during the marriage. And once the divorce was granted, the wife found that her husband had been having an affair with her best friend. With facts like these, most likely she could have gotten custody originally without much of a fight. Due to the wife's naive mistake, the husband now has custody of the child, with the wife seeing the child on a limited basis. The wife now agonizes every day over her bad decision, and her former husband constantly reminds her that he has control over the situation.

This client asked me specifically to tell her story in this book, in the hope that someone else might not make the same tragic mistake. If she had fought for custody of her child, the emotional trauma she is now experiencing would be in the past. In this case, her one bite at the apple was missed. If you foolishly accept whatever settlement your spouse offers without adequate information or advice, you are dealing from a position of weakness — and weakness has never culminated in THE SUCCESSFUL DIVORCE.

*I don't believe man is woman's
natural enemy.
Perhaps his lawyer is.*

Shana Alexander

CHAPTER 5

Hiring Mr. Or Ms. Right

Finding a lawyer is not difficult. There are nearly one million attorneys in the United States and more than 11,000 licensed in the state of Alabama alone. But connecting with a talented expert — one who makes you feel he or she can safeguard your future — is an extremely difficult process. The first requirement is to find a lawyer who concentrates his or her practice in matrimonial law. If you are going to be involved in a contested divorce, you want an attorney who not only knows the law, but what each individual judge prefers and looks at in each case. We use the analogy that no one would want an eye doctor to perform heart surgery. When it comes to the medical profession, everyone is quick to demand a specialist. Divorcing people, though, frequently hire just any attorney. This attorney's specialty may be bankruptcy or another unrelated field. Marriages that have lasted more than one year, with children or complex property arrangements, demand the services of a family law expert.

Finding the "Right" Lawyer

One of the best ways to find a divorce lawyer is to ask divorced people who they used and whether they were pleased with the result. If you know an attorney who practices in a field other than matrimonial law, ask him or her for recommendations. The local bar association may also have a referral service categorizing various attorneys by their specialties. In addition, clergy, counselors, accountants, financial planners and other professionals often can point you in the right direction.

Once you have the names of several attorneys, you will need to schedule initial interviews with one or more of them. When you call an attorney's office, determine what fees you will pay for this initial consultation. Divorce lawyers generally charge by the hour, and you may or may not have to pay a consultation fee for this first meeting. The attorney will want to cover the basic history of the marriage and the issues involved in the divorce at this initial meeting. You should be as candid as possible. Do not make the mistake of thinking your spouse will not bring up certain issues such as adultery, physical abuse, substance abuse or certain sexual practices, when you try to take his or her children or a valued marital asset. The lawyer is under an ethical obligation not to disclose the information you provide unless you consent. But you cannot get an honest evaluation of your case if you have not been completely honest and upfront regarding all of the issues involved. If you are dealing with an expert in matrimonial law, it is doubtful that the facts of your case will shock him.

The lawyer will initially try to determine the basic issues that are likely to be contested and summarize the major assets and debts of the parties. You can aid the lawyer by providing detailed lists of all of the debts and assets of the marriage. In addition, the lawyer may request a narrative summarizing the reasons you want this divorce.

These interviews also should serve to educate you, especially if you are paying for them. You'll want to hear about the types of family law cases each attorney has handled. If a family business or some other valuable marital asset is at stake, you'll want to know the attorney's track record handling complex property arrangements and the resources (accountants, business-oriented expert witnesses) he can call upon in such cases. If children are involved, you may want to speak with clients who've used this attorney's custody services. And most of all, you'll want to determine if the chemistry is there between attorney and client.

You may begin your search wanting the meanest "junk yard dog" in town. But meanness often infers obstructionism. That usually costs money, and in the long run may not lead you to THE SUCCESSFUL DIVORCE. Some cases demand a tough-guy strategy, especially if the other side employs it. But you may decide that an attorney who can successfully settle a case is more to your liking. Matching the attorney to the type of case is essential, for this person will know your deepest, darkest secrets and you will have to work together throughout the process.

At the conclusion of the initial meeting, both you and the attorney will determine whether to proceed further in the matter. If so, the lawyer will give you some homework — a list of additional information required to prepare the case — and you will likely execute an agreement concerning legal fees.

Keeping Fees Down

Most matrimonial law experts charge on an hourly basis for work performed by the lawyer and his staff. In rare cases, a flat fee rather than an hourly fee may be charged for certain limited services. A contested divorce can take a significant amount of time to bring to a successful conclusion. Each time you meet with the lawyer, he works on your case, his staff works on your case or you speak with him on the telephone, additional time and money will be used up if he is working on an hourly basis.

Don't use your attorney as a sounding board for all the "he said, she said" gripes that are common in a contested divorce. Gossiping will cost you money. It makes more sense to write down what you want your attorney to know. If these facts are significant, tell the attorney directly, either in person or on the telephone. But many of the details of divorce are not earth shaking.

Most matrimonial law experts charge a great deal for clients who call them at home or on weekends, just to vent their complaints. This is valuable family time for the attorney, and you should respect his privacy. Instead, talk to the secretary or legal assistant as often as possible. Let your attorney know you are doing that intentionally, so as not to waste his time... and your money. If there is an emergency, though, it may be necessary to call your attorney at home. I make certain every client knows to call me at home if the need arises. But it should be a matter of great urgency, that cannot wait until morning. You and your attorney should agree about what specifically constitutes an emergency.

How combative the opposing party gets can affect the cost of your case. If your spouse wants his or her "day in court," or will not bend on the simplest property issues, you may be in for a lengthy and expensive battle. This type of opposing party will fight everything your attorney attempts to do in the case, resulting in significantly higher legal bills for both sides.

The Initial Retainer

Most family attorneys require a retainer, which is a down payment that ensures the lawyer will be paid for the time incurred in the case. Retainers ranging from $750 to $10,000 are common in most areas of Alabama, although retainers up to $25,000 may be required in very complex cases. The highest retainers usually involve a complicated custody fight or complex property arrangement.

The retainer may only be a partial payment of the fees in the case, depending upon the time involved in completing the action. If the case settles without utilizing the entire retainer, or if the client decides to seek other legal representation, then whatever amount has not been applied to time spent on the case will be returned to the client.

There is a saying in the legal profession that if a client cannot afford to pay the lawyer during the middle of a crisis, it is unlikely the client will pay the lawyer once the problem is solved. It is not unusual for the attorney facing trial to get a supplemental retainer to cover the expenses of being in court. A contested trial may take several days or weeks of trial time to resolve, plus all of the preparation time. Accordingly, you need to financially prepare for all of these expenses. Fees and expenses can be substantial, and the attorney expects to be paid as the services are rendered, just like any other professional.

People often call our office and say, "I don't have any money, and I can't afford to hire you, but can I ask you several questions about my case?" This is similar to calling your doctor and telling him that you have discovered a huge lump and want to know over the phone whether or not it is cancer and how can you remove it yourself. Neither the lawyer nor the doctor can properly advise clients over the phone, based on such limited facts.

If money for a retainer is not readily available, you may have other sources to rely on for payment of these funds. Advances on credit cards, bank notes or a short-term loan from a friend or relative are all possibilities. Most attorneys will not proceed in a case until the retainer is paid. So you may need to explore several options to obtain the necessary funds.

Don't Gamble on Your Spouse
Paying Your Legal Fees

The court may or may not require your spouse to pay your legal fees. If the fees are not awarded to your spouse, or if he or she fails to pay them, you will be responsible for them. Most divorce experts

27

require the client to pay the fees incurred before the case is resolved. Then if the other side is ordered to absorb the fees, the lawyer will reimburse the client once the balance is paid. In most cases, divorce experts will not take on a litigated divorce hoping the other side will pay the fees. However, some attorneys file cases without having been paid a penny, on the mere hope that the other spouse will pay their fees.

Taking the case on that basis usually results in the lawyer not getting paid for a long time, or the client being left with a huge bill he or she hoped the spouse would pay. If your lawyer has done a good job representing you, the other spouse will not be thrilled to pay the attorney's fees of the person who caused him or her so much difficulty.

Often people fail to recognize the enormous amount of money at stake in a divorce, including the cumulative value of child support and alimony, and the related property settlement issues. For example, if a 35-year-old woman requests $1,500 per month in periodic alimony from her husband, the payments could easily total more than half a million dollars over her lifetime. Coupled with child support awards, property settlements, equity in the home, retirement plans, insurance considerations, debts, and college expenses, the value of an estate can range from several hundred thousand dollars to several million dollars in a divorce of middle class people. With that kind of money on the line, hiring a skilled matrimonial law specialist is a prudent investment.

Paying the Lawyer's Hourly Rate: There Are No Contingency Fees

What do you mean I owe you money — the other lawyer's ad I saw on television said you get no money unless you collect.

An Anonymous Client

The Alabama Rules of Professional Conduct prohibit contingency fees in divorce cases except in very limited circumstances. Under a contingency arrangement (oftentimes an accident or injury case), an attorney is paid a percentage of the settlement award. The famous advertisement line that "you will pay no attorney's fees unless we recover" may apply to a personal injury case, but not to the legal fees in your divorce.

Since your divorce attorney will charge either a flat rate or hourly, it's important to find out what the attorney charges for himself, his associates and his staff. Generally, the rule of thumb to follow is an age old one; you get what you pay for. Most matrimonial law experts in Alabama charge from $100 to $250 and upwards per hour for their services, and $50 and up per hour for paralegals and other staff members.

Ask For a Statement

You should be kept abreast of the time incurred in your case and the balance of any retainer. Legal time can quickly add up and surpass the value of the assets in question. If your spouse is being overly difficult, your attorney will invest a lot of time in your case, and your fees will rise quickly. If your attorney does the work, you will be obligated to pay the fees regardless of the outcome. Many clients want the lawyer to do an enormous amount of work without realizing the tremendous costs associated with it.

Preparing a case for trial may require the lawyer to work many hours preparing witnesses for trial. Many clients are quick to say they want their lawyer "to do whatever it takes." This type of attitude can cost an incredible amount of money. And giving your attorney carte blanche authority to spend your money rarely produces THE SUCCESSFUL DIVORCE. This type of client often compares the value of the settlement to the legal bills without considering the services performed by the lawyer. Some lawyers simply tell you the balance due at the end of the divorce. This practice should be avoided, because you may end up with a substantial balance far beyond your expectations. Therefore, make sure to request billing statements if your attorney does not provide them.

Who Is Responsible For Expenses?

Most attorneys bill you separately for expenses incurred in the case, including filing fees and deposition costs. These costs are incurred by the attorney in the course of representation, and are generally due at the time the services are rendered. The average filing fee for a divorce action in Alabama is $116. Deposition costs are generally based on the length of the deposition. The lawyer pays a court reporter to record the testimony in the deposition. A typical divorce deposition will cost anywhere from $300 to $500 or more for the court reporter. This does not include the attorney's time associated with preparing for and taking the deposition.

Another expense is special process server fees. These are charges for serving the opposing party with pleadings, subpoenas and other related documents. If time is important, a special process server can serve the documents immediately, while the local sheriff's department sometimes takes several weeks. The fee for service of documents by a process server generally runs from $50 to $100 or more, depending upon the difficulty incurred in locating and serving the individual. Many law firms charge for copies and faxes as well as other costs associated with preparing the case. It is always wise to familiarize yourself with the anticipated costs to avoid confusion.

What's the Responsibility of the Lawyer, and What is Yours?

If you hire the lawyer after the initial meeting, you should know what steps your attorney plans to take next. For instance, you should know when he expects to file the divorce and when the other spouse will be served with papers. You should be kept abreast of the latest developments in the case, so you will be prepared if your spouse throws out some bit of information about the case. Your spouse may or may not retaliate in response to the divorce action, especially after being served with divorce papers. If the lawyer has a problem advising you of what action he or she will take, it may be an early indication of a communication problem between the lawyer and client which you should address immediately.

In most instances, the attorney will give you homework at the end of your initial meeting. He will need to know everything possible about the marriage and about the reasons for divorce and the overall history of the marriage. This type of narrative can prove extremely helpful to the lawyer and his staff in preparing your case. It should be as detailed as possible. Be careful to prepare this type of information at work or at a safe place where your spouse cannot find it. For example, a detailed history of your ongoing adulterous relationship would be extremely damaging if your spouse discovered it. Also, the lawyer probably will need a detailed listing of assets and debts. And if custody is an issue, the lawyer will need extensive information on the children.

People going through a divorce often suffer from a Humpty Dumpty syndrome, thinking that the lawyers or judge can put their lives back together. The most anyone can hope for is to be left with the tools to do it themselves.

An Alabama Circuit Court Judge

CHAPTER 6

When Mr. Right Becomes
The Wrong Attorney For You

If you aren't going to get along with your attorney in a divorce, you will know about it very soon.

Larry Upshaw, a writer from Dallas, Texas who lectures attorneys on improving their image before the public, says that all over the country, inattention to detail is the greatest problem clients have with their attorneys.

He Doesn't Return Your Phone Calls

Upshaw tells the story of two friends, one a divorce attorney and the other needing a divorce. Sounds like a good combination. At least he thought so when he brought them together.

That was before the attorney went for months, not returning repeated telephone calls from the client, who simply wanted to know about the progress of her case. Soon she gave up expecting the attorney to call her back and began to ask for the legal assistant. The assistant continually referred her to the attorney, so the client was reduced to begging for news from the receptionist.

After more than six months had elapsed and the client had no notice that a divorce was filed, she began to send faxes and then letters to the attorney. Almost in a panic, she began to get creative. Telling the receptionist that it was she, the client, who had failed to call back the attorney, she wrangled the attorney's car phone number out of the receptionist. After several tries, she got him en route.

Without skipping a beat, the attorney said things were beginning to happen and that he was on his way to the courthouse on some vague matter dealing with her divorce.

"And I've been meaning to call you because we have a settlement offer from the other side," said the attorney.

"What does it say?" asked the client.

"I don't know," replied the attorney. "I haven't read it."

This is not the type of communication that results in THE SUCCESSFUL DIVORCE.

Excitement Versus Cost

Sometimes an excited client can stir an attorney into too much action, resulting in a lot of wasted motion and money and, finally, an angry client.

Larry Upshaw tells about a noted physician who shopped around for "the meanest lawyer in town" to take on his soon-to-be ex-wife, whom he called a "crazy woman." When he found a divorce lawyer with his same glint of revenge in his eye, he retained the man and paid him a $10,000 retainer for a complex divorce with children involved.

Soon the "paper was flying" in the form of a divorce petition and numerous motions that contained all manner of accusations about his wife and the mother of his children. When the client called the attorney's office, he was put through immediately. The client would engage the attorney in long, rambling conversations raging against his ex. The attorney was even called by the client on the weekend, including calls to his cellular number and his lake house.

With all of that action, the client had to replenish the retainer with another $10,000, then $5,000 more. But things were starting to happen. His in-laws, who were close to him before all of this, would not speak to him. And his children were so upset that he had to pay for counseling. The doctor's practice was suffering an unusual number of appointment cancellations, and the level of tension was so high that the client had trouble sleeping.

Soon the client had enough. When he called to complain, the attorney reminded him that he said to "spare no expense," " be aggressive" and "make the other side miserable."

"But I also said to win," said the client. "I've spent $25,000 and I'm farther away from winning than I was when I started."

The client eventually learned the hard way about winning at "all cost." He began to allow the lawyer to handle the case in the proper, methodical fashion. Once the tensions calmed, the parties were eventually able to settle the case. The moral of this story is that you need to follow your lawyer's advice and not set out to destroy the other side. I always tell clients that I won't tell them how to do their job as long as they won't tell me how to practice law.

Evaluate Your Lawyer's Performance

Clients should constantly evaluate their lawyer's performance by these benchmarks: are you closer to a resolution of the divorce than you were when you hired him? Do you feel that you'll get anywhere close to what he suggested you would get? Will you and the other side be able to deal with each other when the case is over? How much is this costing you?

At the same time, you must understand that your lawyer is not a magician. He cannot create miracles and if your spouse is difficult, the fees will increase. If nothing is happening in the case, you should not expect daily or weekly updates. Relaying such information will use up your retainer needlessly.

But if it becomes apparent that the lawyer is not making progress, you may have to consider replacing your attorney with another. This is a drastic move, one you should make only after careful consideration. It can be expensive to constantly change attorneys, and oftentimes we find that people who change attorneys simply have unrealistic expectations. Changing attorneys without a very good reason can create the impression that the client is the difficult person, not the lawyer. But if you have made up your mind, making the change should not be difficult.

Simply call your lawyer and discuss your concerns in detail. If you want to get another attorney, call or write your attorney and ask him or her to send your file to you or another attorney. If you cannot reach him by phone, send him a fax or letter and call his office to confirm it. For the good of your case, it is best not to make the change when you are facing an immediate court appearance.

But whenever this happens, you should receive a refund of any retainer amount being held by the retiring attorney, or pay any existing balance due, subject to the terms of your written fee agreement.

NOTES:

PART TWO

The Heart of the Case

Lawyer: *Are you married?*
Witness: *No, I'm divorced.*
Lawyer: *And what did your husband
            do before you divorced him?*
Witness: *A lot of things I didn't
            know about.*

CHAPTER 7

How to Win at Trial Before it Begins

How aggressively you should pursue your divorce is always a point of debate. If you come on too strong, you might alienate someone you've lived with and loved. If you approach the divorce meekly, you may be setting yourself up to be run over.

A Little Assertiveness

Given these two choices, to err on the side of assertive action usually is the best way to reach THE SUCCESSFUL DIVORCE. If some piece of property belongs to you, you need to talk to your attorney about whether you need to get it out of the house. If your spouse's behavior endangers the children, and you can prove it, you also need to discuss with your attorney how to protect you and the children during the pendency of the case. Decisions like these should always be made after consulting with your attorney.

In a contested divorce, you must obtain as much information about the marriage as possible before your spouse is served notice of the divorce. A wealth of information is kept at home that can make or break your case at trial. Begin immediately to accumulate as much information as possible regarding your financial affairs, as well as

41

who is at fault for the divorce, without raising the suspicions of your spouse.

Obtain Family Information

Locating certain kinds of family information may help you establish crucial key evidence at trial. Obtain the past three to five years of the following information:

- Family photographs relevant to a custody battle
- Incriminating photographs - even if the other spouse is in the photo
- Love letters from your spouse to a third party
- Love letters from a third party to your spouse
- Any "secrets" of yours
- Any "secrets" of your spouse
- Personal tax returns
- Corporate tax returns
- Checking and savings account statements
- Financial records
- Medical records
- Substance abuse evidence or treatment records
- Brokerage or stock accounts
- Retirement account statements
- Mortgage information
- Credit card information
- Personal debt information
- Telephone records
- Long-distance telephone bills
- Cellular telephone bills
- Health insurance information
- Life insurance information
- Any other important financial information

This information may or may not be used at trial, but if possible it should be placed in a safe location inaccessible to your spouse. If any of these records can damage your spouse's case, they may "disappear" if you don't have them in hand once the divorce is initiated.

If your spouse pays for his girlfriend's hotel room with a credit card, the last thing he and his attorney will want is for that receipt to show up in court. Although adultery is not as important in the divorce process of some states, it is still relevant in Alabama and can be a major factor for consideration of custody, alimony and property division determinations. Keep whatever information you have in a safe place, because it may have to be turned over to the other side's attorney during the course of the litigation.

You should not construe this section as advising you to hide any information or assets, or that you will ultimately receive all of the assets just because you have them in your possession. On the contrary, you need be as forthright as possible in the manner in which you handle your case. However, if you hold the vast majority of the key evidence at the beginning of the case, you will be much more in control. The following discussion summarizes how some of this information can be used to your advantage or against you at trial, depending on the facts of your case.

Financial Records

Many financial records contain a wealth of information that only one spouse knows. For example, most bank accounts normally show paycheck deposits on the first and fifteenth of each month. However, a spouse may deposit substantially more money in his checking account on a monthly basis. The origin of these funds will help to indicate that spouse's true monthly income.

Most likely, a spouse will claim his only income is his base salary. But if he repeatedly deposits $25,000 a month in his account, while only earning $10,000 per month, the history of the additional funds may be used to indicate additional income. This may indicate large commissions or bonuses that he is receiving on a regular basis. It may indicate a likely source of considerable debt, or a gambling problem, if the spouse has been taking advances from credit cards and other loans to meet monthly expenses.

Long Distance and Cellular Phone Records

Long distance and cellular phone records may prove helpful to show an adulterous relationship. It is effective at trial to enlarge a long distance phone statement with page after page of calls to the same unexplained number. Once you identity the person being called, the lawyer simply poses the question, "What did you talk to Jane Doe about for seven hours from your car in one day?" "Is that phone sex?" Likewise, calls to illicit 900 sexual fantasy numbers can be very damaging at trial. Most divorce lawyers will request both personal and business cellular phone and long distance records for the past three to five years. Therefore, if a spouse has been hiding certain calls behind his business accounts, the information will prove very valuable and the guilty spouse may want to settle the case to keep his employer from finding out about the adulterous relationship. This may be especially true if the records indicate that the spouse has been having the affair on company time.

Your Secrets

While gathering incriminating evidence on a spouse, you also need to consider any evidence about yourself. There are two kinds of client evidence likely to be harmful at trial. The first is the kind the other spouse knows about, such as illegal drugs, incriminating photographs, sexual paraphernalia, videotapes and adulterous love letters, etc. The other is the kind of evidence the other spouse doesn't know about but can "dig up," if given a chance.

Your spouse may not have concrete evidence of an adulterous relationship but may attempt to obtain such evidence through a private investigator or standard discovery procedures, such as interrogatories and depositions. It may be too late if your spouse already has this information. You should, however, make every effort to prevent this evidence from being found prematurely by your spouse. Otherwise, you may give away facts that will damage your case.

I remember one client's spouse who was foolish enough to write checks for all of his girlfriend's bills from the joint account and even write on the checks that they were for "Sharon's rent," "Sharon's clothes," etc. Needless to say, he had a lot of explaining to do at trial when he denied an adulterous relationship and said he did not know anyone named Sharon.

For some strange reason, people who are having affairs act similar to a 16-year-old who is in love for the first time. The spouse having the affair abandons all logic and does some of the dumbest things in the name of love. Many people will go to restaurants with a girlfriend or boyfriend, forgetting that the other spouse's friends may also be present. Also, taking that person to lunch during the work week usually gives a secretary or other coworker knowledge of the person's whereabouts. They write love letters and leave them in a briefcase or purse. They will also take pictures of each other together, and sometimes they begin buying new things such as lingerie or sexual devices.

Not-So Secrets

I remember one particular case in which a 50-year-old husband began going to a tanning salon, working out, buying new red underwear and working late every night. It did not take long for the wife to become suspicious of his activities. She determined that he had been going out of town and booking plane tickets in the girlfriend's name, calling the girlfriend daily on his cellular phone, charging local hotel bills on his credit card and writing checks to the girlfriend from their joint account. The wife discovered most of this information before we got involved in the case. As difficult as it was to keep this secret, she did so until after we had filed a complaint for divorce and made every effort to protect her and the marital assets.

If you are having an affair, do not assume that you are so good at it that no one will ever know. If you are meeting your lover on a regular basis, most talented private investigators can and will catch you. If the police can catch professional criminals, it does not take a rocket scientist to catch a person going to the local motel with a girlfriend or boyfriend.

If you have been having an affair and the divorce is initiated, stop immediately. An amazing number of people seem compelled to continue seeing a paramour, even when they know their spouse is having them followed. Sometimes it's as if the spouse wants to get caught, because he or she is so blatantly foolish. If you insist on continuing the relationship, just make sure it's worth the check you will have to write when the divorce is over.

If there are documents that might prove the existence of an affair by your spouse, you need to obtain the originals whenever possible. Your lawyer may or may not be able to get copies of key evidence admitted at trial, due to certain evidentiary limitations. You must balance the fact that your spouse will likely become very suspicious when certain things disappear. I have often advised clients not to worry about uncovering their spouse's secrets and angering them. It is doubtful the spouse will come out and say, "Honey, have you seen the naked pictures of my girlfriend. I was hiding them right here in my briefcase?"

Please be aware, however, that if violence is a possibility, be cautious if you start removing incriminating bits of evidence from your spouse's hiding places. The determination of how and when to get the evidence must be made on a case-by-case basis and should be made with the advice of your attorney.

Evidence of Sexual Misconduct

Clients have to recognize that during a divorce, evidence can be viewed in more than one way. For example, the most innocent and fun videotape or photograph of a "sexual encounter" with your spouse or paramour can become some of the most damaging evidence in a custody trial. Likewise, copies of phone bills with repeated calls to 900 sex line numbers could enhance the opposing side's position in a custody battle. Unless you can show that this type of conduct adversely affects the children, however, it may not be as effective at trial as you hoped. Be sure to discuss this evidence with your lawyer, so he can determine what should be done with it.

Just because a spouse was involved in a particular sexual escapade does not always produce a "slam dunk" at trial for the other side. If both parties participated in a kinky episode involving some unusual sexual practice, the court is likely to hold both parties equally responsible and may not put too much weight on the activity unless the children were present. This is due primarily to the fact that since both parties were willing participants, it is not fair to hold one party at fault for something that both parties participated in on a regular basis. Of course, the argument at trial usually centers around the fact that "I didn't want to do that and he made me do it." Again, if the parties have done this activity for years, that may be a hard argument to sell. If, however, a spouse has forced another to participate in activities that the other spouse did not want to participate in, such as the use of some kind of sexual device or some kind of forced sex, the court may not look kindly on the forcing spouse.

Photographs and Other Documentation of Abusive Incidents

In a divorce trial, a picture is definitely worth a thousand words. If a spouse is in an abusive situation, such abuse must be documented with photographs and medical reports which can be shown at trial. If an abusive spouse has left his wife or children bruised and beaten, these marks will be gone long before trial. Pictures of each bruise or abrasion should be taken immediately and medical treatment secured from an attending physician. Police reports should be made after consulting with your lawyer. You may have difficulty convincing a judge that the abuse took place if there are no photographs, medical records or police reports. Also, police officers and friends can be subpoenaed to testify to events they have witnessed.

There are many violent marriages that involve men who should be punished for their behavior. This type of behavior should not be tolerated. In most cases, the abused spouse exhibits such fear of the man that a long history of abuse is apparent. However, some women say their husbands were abusive during the marriage, yet they don't want to hurt their feelings by having them arrested.

Clients like this rarely want a restraining order or to have the husband forcibly removed from the home. In fact, often they will continue sexual relations with the "abusive spouse." Some people may act this way out of fear. But I believe certain people exaggerate the level of abuse they have incurred in an attempt to better their case. This is a dangerous ploy that has no place in the divorce process. If you plead abuse to your attorney, you need to make certain that such abuse has occurred and you can back it up with witnesses, photographs and police reports. If you lie about it at trial, this type of behavior will definitely affect your case. So many people have lied about abuse in the past that the court is now automatically skeptical and requires significant proof to substantiate the abuse.

Hiring a Private Investigator

Do not hire a private investigator without first calling your attorney. The attorney will likely have an investigator he trusts and recommends for your case. Unless the attorney hires the private investigator, the work may not be protected by the attorney/client privilege, and it may be more easily discoverable by the other side. In certain cases, especially those involving adultery or income questions, a private investigator can prove to be the most important aspect of the case. If the investigator is successful in catching your spouse with a girlfriend or boyfriend, photographs and videotape may win your case. You can imagine the judge's reaction when you produce large photographs at trial of your spouse kissing the person that he or she just testified to have never met. Perhaps one of the greatest private investigator stories was told to me by a fellow attorney. This attorney's investigator caught a mother in an adulterous relationship, having sex on videotape. The videotape went on to show the mother having sex in a car, with the mother's young son beside them in the car seat. Obviously, this tape was very damaging to the mother's case at trial.

Depending on the evidence in your case, the private investigator's report may be repetitive and simply back up evidence you already have. It may not add to the substance of your case. In addition, a private investigator will likely charge on an hourly basis. The investigator may follow your spouse for several days, which will result in a substantial expense. The cost of this investigation will be due immediately, regardless of whether the investigator has found any incriminating evidence. Remember that a skillful trial lawyer can discredit many private investigators' reports due to flaws in their actions or experience as a investigator. As a result, many people throw away money on a private investigator's report that may not add to the substance of the case.

Tape Recorders

Before you hook up a tape recorder to your telephone, consult with your attorney. Strict laws protect people from being taped without their knowledge. Violation of these laws can result in criminal penalties and potentially damage your case. In limited circumstances, the tape recording of a conversation may be admissible if you are a party to that conversation. If you are not a party to that conversation, the tape almost always is inadmissible and illegal.

Many judges do not like to deal with tape recordings of the other spouse during a divorce trial. They tend to view them as a devious form of spying on the other side. However, due to the tendency of the other spouse to deny certain incriminating matters, a tape recording may be your only way to establish the truth. If your spouse has been mentally or physically abusive toward you or your children, a tape recording can be damaging at trial — if the abusive spouse denies the incident occurred. Determining whether to use a tape recording should be made on a case-by-case basis. Certain cases warrant taping when there is no other way to establish certain points at trial. If you already have the other party on tape admitting a certain fact, it is very difficult for them to deny it at trial.

Evidence About You

Anyone going through a divorce should assume the other side is collecting the same kind of evidence they are gathering. Many cases have been lost because a spouse thought "my spouse does not have a clue about what I've done." In reality, that spouse had several clues, and also got several pieces of evidence due to the client's foolish mistakes. To reemphasize the point made earlier, it is imperative for you to be completely honest with your attorney about what you have done.

I can recall every client who has directly lied to me about a particular issue. If a client denied an adulterous relationship and is then shown in a video in bed with his paramour, we have a problem. Usually, our only recourse is to withdraw from representing the lying client. To avoid this problem, tell your lawyer the truth as early and often as possible.

Your quest for THE SUCCESSFUL DIVORCE continues through the

pendency of the case. Your life, in essence, does not begin until the final judgment of divorce is signed by the judge. If a divorce is pending, don't give the other side more ammunition. You need to behave and not be in a hurry to begin dating. In fact, the best rule to follow is "don't do anything." Don't fight, don't drink, don't date, don't do anything that your mother or minister would not condone. Many clients say "it isn't fair that my spouse gets to have an affair and I cannot even go out to dinner while this divorce is pending." I do not care if it is an innocent dinner date with your best friend of the opposite sex during the pendency of the divorce. It should not happen. You do not want the other side's lawyer bringing up the date at trial. First, it is impossible to convince a judge that you are upset about the breakup of the marriage when you are already dating.

If custody is at issue, you do not want the other side asserting that while he or she was at home keeping the children, you were out drinking in a bar with someone. Even the most innocent situation with your "good friend" can certainly be construed in a negative light. Trust me — a talented divorce lawyer with a little ammunition can make Mary Poppins look unfit.

The other side wants to cloud the issues in an attempt to detract from their fault at trial. Your spouse may know you are not having an affair. But if he is having one, you can bet he is going to try to show you are also guilty of dating, to minimize the harm caused by his adulterous relationship. Plenty of clients have won their cases, only to lose them by their actions during the pendency of the divorce. If this happens, please make certain you are represented by the other side and not by my office!

Establishing Household Needs?

Appendix A includes a sample budget form that should help you determine your expenses. The expenses listed on the form must be supported by receipts and documentation at trial to show their validity. It is important to balance your needs with your wants and desires. For example, most couples cannot afford to live together, much less split the expenses of two separate households. Even if you think you must live in a mansion, you may have to adjust your standard of living to deal with the realities of divorce.

From this information, you should be able to estimate your present and future expenses. A lawyer needs these before he can determine the financial support necessary for your future welfare or your ability to pay support to your spouse. Often, this is a difficult challenge, because many clients are not familiar with the family finances.

Lawyer: *What is your name?*
Witness: *Ernestine McDowell.*
Lawyer: *And what is your marital status?*
Witness: *Fair.*

CHAPTER 8

Mediation

One of the best pathways to THE SUCCESSFUL DIVORCE may lie in mediation. Over the past decade, there has been a trend toward alternative dispute resolution all across the country. Today, there are mediators who do only family mediation, while others handle family and business disputes.

It's Usually Voluntary

In some jurisdictions, families must submit to mediation before the court will hear the divorce case. In Alabama, mediation is usually voluntary. If either side requests it, though, and is willing to pay for it, mediation will be ordered in certain types of cases.

Mediation usually is not binding on the parties, unless a settlement agreement is signed. But it has great advantages in those cases where the parties can see a middle ground. Using mediation to settle a divorce case can be less expensive, because you avoid most of the discovery process, preparation for trial and the actual time in court. Should the mediation process not be successful, the parties have only lost a minimal amount of time and money in comparison to the potential costs of protracted litigation. Successful mediation, however, oftentimes leaves the parties much more pleased with the outcome because they reached it on their own, rather than having it forced on them by a judge.

In many ways, mediation is a form of the same settlement process attorneys have engaged in since the judicial system began. Still, you have the two attorneys present as advocates for their clients. The major difference is that with mediation, the parties and their attorneys are placed in separate rooms, and a neutral trained mediator helps the parties to resolve their differences.

The Mediator's Job

The mediator acts as the connecting point, relaying areas of agreement between the parties and feeling the parties out on some areas where disagreement could turn into a settlement. Generally, the parties will submit to the mediator all of the pertinent pleadings, financial documents, depositions, and related evidence about the case to help the mediator understand the issues in the case. The mediator then begins to work with the parties to attempt to help them resolve the disputed issues. In many complex cases, the mediation may take more than one day to finalize. If, at the end of the day, an agreement is reached, the lawyers formalize it into a settlement agreement that the parties then execute and file with the court.

The main advantage of mediation is that it settles some cases, thereby reducing the logjam at the courthouse. And even when it doesn't work, it leaves people with the feeling that they tried the most rational means before submitting to the more abrasive court process.

Knowledge is of two kinds. We know a subject ourselves, or we know where we can find information upon it.

Samuel Johnson

CHAPTER 9

Relevant Information:
Building a Strong Case

There are three sides to every divorce case — his side, her side and the truth.

An Alabama Circuit Court Judge

The process of formal discovery gives both parties the ability to obtain additional information from the other side concerning the relevant issues in the case. These discovery procedures involve formal legal procedures in which one side is required to respond to specific requests made by the opposing party. These procedures may include written interrogatories, requests for production of documents, request for admissions, depositions and other forms of examination. In a perfect world, the parties should be able to exchange any relevant documents without the necessity of a formal request. In a divorce, it is fairly common that one side will have to force the other side to provide even basic information such as checking account statements and tax returns.

Discovery is an essential part of the divorce process, except with an uncontested divorce or where the marriage has been extremely short with few assets. If you realize your spouse had other assets or fault after the divorce is final, it usually won't matter if you had an opportunity to discover this information and failed to do so. Remember, you only get one bite at the apple — make sure it is a good one.

This information may prove to be helpful to your case. At the same time, however, you may incur considerable expense in forcing your spouse to respond to the discovery requests. Many clients mistakenly believe this information is not necessary or that it would be too expensive to obtain, but then want to blame the attorney for not discovering all the marital assets.

The following discussion briefly summarizes the basic forms of discovery your lawyer may utilize during your case.

Interrogatories

Interrogatories consist of a series of written questions designed to discover certain facts regarding the case from the opposing party. Answers to the interrogatories must be prepared and filed within a prescribed period of time and the answers are given under oath. Many people fail to realize that the court does not look favorably upon a party who lies in the interrogatory responses. If a party is shown during the trial to have lied, the case may be greatly affected. At the same time, don't expect the judge to be in total shock if it is shown that the other side was less than truthful. Unfortunately, many spouses lie on a regular basis during their divorce, and it may be difficult to get the court to punish the responsible party.

The interrogatories usually involve questions related to a party's employment and salary information, bank account information, charge accounts, assets, debts, etc. There may be questions concerning whether or not an adulterous relationship has taken place during the marriage. The other side may ask about abuse of a spouse or children, use of illegal drugs, etc. If any of the fault questions are applicable to you, you need to discuss the questions with your attorney to determine the best way to handle the response. The answers also will have to be updated prior to trial, if there are any changes.

Request for Production of Documents

A request for production of documents is often served at the same time as the interrogatories are served upon the opposing party. The requests contain specific demands for certain documents needed for the preparation of the case. The requesting party usually wants three to five years worth of bank statements, tax returns, charge statements, business records, insurance information, financial data and numerous other kinds of information, including any evidence that the party plans to use at trial.

This information will be examined to determine the relevant issues in question. If the information is not given to the other side, this may prevent either side from using it at trial. There is no quicker way to impact the other side at trial than to object to the admission of a key piece of evidence because it was not listed in the party's responses to the request for production. If it was properly requested and the other side simply failed to answer, the court will likely prevent the use of the evidence at trial. Also, the request for production of documents, like the interrogatories, must be answered within a specified period of time and updated prior to trial.

Request for Admissions

Requests for admissions contain questions in which the opposing party must admit or deny a fact in the case. These requests are used to shortcut the discovery process to immediately determine the opposing party's fault in the case. For example, the attorney may ask the opposing party to admit or deny an extramarital affair during the marriage. A guilty party is put in a delicate situation when asked this question. To admit the adultery may concede a fact that the other side would have trouble proving at trial. If you deny the adultery and the other side is successful in proving it at trial, you will not only have committed adultery, but also perjury. In addition, there are strict time limits for answering a request for admission. A failure to answer the requests for admission in a timely fashion may cause the requests to be deemed admitted by the trial court. Therefore, the opposing party cannot simply avoid answering the questions without additional consequences.

Depositions

In many divorce cases, a deposition is necessary to find out the basis of the opposing party's case or the substance of the testimony of a witness in the case. A deposition is taken out of court, under oath, in the presence of a court reporter. Usually it is taken at one of the lawyer's offices. The lawyer taking the deposition usually will ask the other side critical questions about the facts of the case and the history of the marriage. A deposition may or may not break your case at trial, depending on the particular facts of your case. For example, your spouse may attempt to determine each and every aspect of your case. You must be prepared for your deposition, so that you do not forget critical parts of the case under the pressure and intensity of a deposition. You must be prepared to name each and every reason you want the divorce at that time, if you plan to utilize it at trial. There are numerous strategies for handling a deposition, and your attorney should advise you about the impact of a particular deposition on your case.

Also, a deposition can be used to discredit a witness if he changes his testimony at trial. Good lawyers use the deposition process to "size up" the opposing party and their case to determine how they will appear on the witness stand. It is important to prepare for the initial deposition and then remember at trial what was said in the deposition. Lawyers often try to trick the other side at trial by stating "that's not what you said at your deposition." Many times the lawyer himself does not remember what the opposing party said in the deposition, but simply wants to test the witness' memory of the deposition. If the lawyer believes the witness was lying, he may attempt to confuse the witness in hopes that he could not remember which story he gave in the deposition.

Certain cases warrant a deposition and other cases do not. Each deposition requires a court reporter and results in additional expense, such as the lawyer's preparation time. Before you begin the deposition process, be certain that it's necessary and that settlement is not possible. Since the deposition will cost several hundred dollars or more for the court reporter, plus the lawyer's time in preparing for and taking the deposition, it is not uncommon for some lengthy depositions to cost from five hundred to several thousand dollars.

If the issue at hand involves a bank account with a minimal amount of money in it, a deposition may not be worth the expenses incurred regardless of whatever information is gathered. If the assets are not known or if custody is at issue, a deposition will likely be necessary unless the information can be obtained through other means.

Snow White doesn't marry Hitler,
and no one party
is 100% at fault.

Anonymous divorce attorney

CHAPTER 10

Who's at Fault?

Alabama does not have an actual no-fault divorce statute, and so the fault of the parties in the breakup of the marriage is a factor in determining the division of marital property and in making an award of custody. If a divorce is uncontested, however, one party can allege incompatibility, and this basically serves as a form of no-fault divorce.

Judges Must Decide

Most divorce court judges in Alabama would rather not have to consider fault. Imagine yourself in their position, listening day after day to the squabbling and fighting of *supposed* adults. They hear highly personal matters in open court. Most judges would rather that cases settle. But under Alabama law, they may use fault as a basis for property division and the awarding of alimony or custody.

If there is no fault present and the parties have merely grown apart, the court usually will attempt to equitably divide the assets and debts of the parties. "Equitable division" is part of Alabama law, one of 40 states with this provision. (The remaining 10 states have community property statutes). Be aware, however, that equitable division does not mean equal division.

The judge determines, based on the facts, what kind of division is fair and equitable. If one spouse has been primarily responsible for the breakup of the marriage, the court has the discretion to compensate the other spouse with a greater division of the property or by awarding alimony. At the same time, one spouse will not necessarily receive the lion's share of the marital assets simply because there is fault. This will depend upon numerous factors including the type of fault, the length of the marriage and the assets and debts in question.

Types of Fault

The following list summarizes the kinds of "fault" often considered by the trial court in a divorce:

- Adultery
- Drug use
- Alcoholism
- Physical abuse of a spouse
- Mental abuse of a spouse
- Physical abuse of a child
- Mental abuse of a child
- Sexual abuse of a child
- Gambling
- Excessive spending
- Mental illness and psychological problems
- Criminal convictions
- Unusual sexual practices

Fault Must Be Proven

Keep in mind that the fault of another party must be proven to a judge in court. You may believe your spouse has been having an affair. When asked what evidence you have about the affair, you cannot simply respond, "Oh, you know he's been sleeping with her, he just acts like he has." You are going to need more than a gut feeling to establish the facts in a courtroom. On the other hand, you will not likely catch your spouse actually in bed with another person. The courts often utilize what is referred to as a "reasonable person's standard," weighing the cumulative effect of all the evidence. The judge often asks whether the evidence indicates the behavior of a married person properly executing familial duties. Most married people are not seen in bars late at night with another person of the opposite sex. Few are found to be at that same person's apartment several times each week and to have hundreds of cellular phone calls to the person late at night. In this type of situation, most divorce lawyers put the burden on the accused party to explain all of these circumstances. Remember, your judge is likely going to be married and have a keen sense of what actions are reasonable and unreasonable in a marriage.

If you are guilty, you need to consider how your actions will look. You and your lawyer can decide how to handle these issues. If you think your spouse is guilty, you need to develop concrete proof to establish guilt and not just rely on speculation and rumor, which are not admissible as evidence at trial.

Marriages don't last. When I meet a guy, the first question I ask myself is: "Is this the man I want my children to spend their weekends with?"

Comedian Rita Rudner

CHAPTER 11

Who Gets the Children?

We have a policy at my office that regardless of what brought the parents into the divorce arena, the children are not at fault. We will not participate in a case if our client insists on badgering the children.

When minor children are involved, the custody of those children is of paramount importance in the divorce. The law surrounding custody is very stringent, and drastically affects the rights of the parties in the future. Every parent always wants to know the answer to the question, "Will I get my children in the divorce?" Sometimes the issue is moot, because one of the parties has already conceded the other spouse custody of the minor children.

The Fight of Your Life

But when custody is contested, you had better prepare for the fight of your life. Nothing is more contentious than a full-blown custody battle. Until recently, women almost automatically received custody of the children, especially infant children. But times are changing, and in many Alabama jurisdictions, men are walking into the courtroom on a more level playing field in a custody fight. Because of these changing times, men are winning custody of the kids in increasing numbers.

Each custody case is unique due to the facts, circumstances, and fault surrounding the breakup of the marriage, as well as each parent's individual relationship and role with the children during and after the marriage.

Retaliation

Many fathers fight for custody simply to retaliate against the mother or to force her to settle the financial issues rather than risk a trial over custody. Some women threaten fathers with limited visitation to gain an economic advantage, or they fraudulently claim sexual abuse of the children to ensure that they get custody. Most spouses can determine whether the other spouse is "serious" about receiving custody. If so, the issue needs to be taken seriously throughout the entire divorce process.

Traditionally, the non-custodial parent's role with the children after the divorce usually mirrors that parent's role before the divorce. If the marriage was a traditional one, where the father spent less time with the children than his wife prior to the divorce, it is doubtful that he will instantly become heavily involved in the children's lives. But if this was a two-wage-earner family, as most are these days, both mother and father probably had their absentee periods. After divorce, it is likely that this relationship will continue. Despite what caused the divorce, the children are not at fault for the breakup and deserve to have the best relationship possible with both parents after the divorce. In addition, the non-custodial parent is more likely to pay child support and help with other expenses related to the child if he or she sees the children regularly.

"The impact of the divorce on the children continues to affect me," says an Alabama Circuit Court Judge. "The children deserve to continue to have two parents."

Types of Custody

The court awards two kinds of custody: sole custody and joint custody. Most divorcing couples misunderstand these custody terms and what each spouse's rights are under the custody arrangement. Initially, you might think joint custody is a great idea. You may change your mind once the arrangement is explained to you. It is sad and ironic how many people call me after they have signed their divorce papers and want to change the custody terms, because their lawyer did not explain the terms to them. The following summarizes the differences between joint and sole custody and the rights of the parents under each.

What is Sole Custody?

Under a sole custody arrangement, one parent has the legal right to the care, custody and control of the minor children. The other parent is awarded specific visitation rights with the children. This means the children will live with the parent who is awarded sole custody. That parent will have the right to make all major decisions related to the children, including medical, educational, academic, and social matters. And they will have the responsibility for those facets of the children's lives.

Standard Visitation

Some parents seem to forget that their children are not like furniture that can be moved in and out of a house without concern. The court tries to stabilize the children, sometimes at the expense of the parents' comfort, setting up a "standard visitation" schedule. Many custodial parents have problems allowing the other parent to have even this minimum visitation with the children.

The court wants to foster the relationship of the children with the non-custodial parent. Unless you can prove that seeing this parent will harm the children, usually the judge will not restrict or limit the non-custodial parent's visitation beyond the standard visitation schedule. The court generally provides three separate visitation schedules, depending on the age of the children. The courts have determined that visitation should vary for children under 12 months of age, from one year to three years and over three years of age. The complete visitation schedules are listed in Appendix E. The schedules may differ slightly for each jurisdiction. You should consult your attorney for the specific language applicable to you.

Standard Out-of-State Visitation

If the non-custodial parent lives out of state, the parties may select or be awarded out-of-state visitation due to the difficulty following the above standard visitation schedules. The out-of-state schedule is primarily tailored to those situations where long distance and airline travel is required. This schedule is described in more detail in the appendix section of this book.

What is Joint Custody?

Joint custody once was considered a panacea for all the ills brought on by divorce. In theory, joint custody allows both parents to retain some control over the children's lives. In addition, it alleviates the stigma many parents feel when they give up custody of their children, or have it taken away by the courts. Alabama recently passed a joint custody statute which authorizes the courts to award joint custody to both parents if it is in the best interest of the children. But don't confuse the legal designation of joint custody with actual, physical joint custody.

In many ways, joint custody in this state is similar to sole custody. Usually it creates a myriad of problems surrounding the care and control of the children. As a result, most judges and divorce attorneys do not like joint custody and only recommend it in limited circumstances where the parents are likely to agree on post-divorce issues.

Under a joint custody arrangement, one parent usually is designated the primary custodian and the other parent is the secondary custodian. The children live with the primary custodian except for the time they visit the other parent under a specified schedule. Traditionally, most joint custody arrangements specify that both parents make joint decisions concerning the children.

But most agreements also specify that when the parents cannot agree on academic, medical, religious and other issues, one party has the final say. This veto power is necessary to resolve disputed issues. Therefore, the parent with the final authority on a particular issue may override the other parent's request every time. For obvious reasons, this veto power can create tremendous conflict in post-divorce situations. For example, the primary custodial parent often retains final authority for academic decisions, since the child lives with that parent. The secondary custodial parent has the right to a voice in academic decisions, but the primary custodian has the final say on disputed issues. If a dispute arises concerning whether the children shall attend public or private schools, the parent with the authority over the academic decisions will have the right to make the final decision. In other words, that parent has the right to say no every time.

One of the primary reasons many family law experts do not favor joint custody is that it tends to push parents together in a false sense of cooperation. This degree of cooperation may be possible between two married parents, but generally couples getting a divorce have little or no ability to agree on even the simplest issues. Furthermore, the label of joint custody often creates a misconception between parents who do not understand their actual legal rights under the custody arrangement. Many parents believe joint custody means that both parents retain an equal 50/50 "vote" in the decisions concerning the children. This is far from the truth and can lead to a shocking realization after the divorce. Joint custody only works for parents who have a good relationship with their children and are willing to make sacrifices to enrich their children's lives.

Sample Joint Custody Language and Visitation Provisions

The following language contains the typical terms contained in a joint custody agreement. Pay particular attention to this language, and if you will apply this to your real life scenarios, you will see the host of potential problems that could arise.

It is agreed by the parties that it is in the best interest of the children, Kate Doe and Jack Doe, for their care, custody and control, to be shared by both parties. The husband and wife understand that shared custody means both parties shall retain full parental rights and responsibilities with respect to their children, regardless of which party has physical custody at any particular time. The husband and wife agree that shared custody means shared parental responsibility and requires both parents to confer so that major decisions affecting the health and welfare of the children will be jointly determined. (Either party can be designated as the primary custodian, but this example assumes the wife is the primary custodian.)

(A) Schedule. The wife shall be the primary custodian and shall maintain the primary residence for the children, and the husband shall be the secondary custodian and shall maintain the secondary residence for the children. The secondary custodian's custodial periods shall be as follows:

(1) The first and third weekends of each month from 6 p.m. on Friday until 6 p.m. the following Sunday. The first weekend shall begin on the first Friday of each month at 6 p.m.;

(2) Each Christmas Day from 3 p.m. until 3 p.m. on the following New Year's Day;

(3) Thirty-one days during the summer (to be taken between June 10 and August 15) to be selected by the non-custodial parent, but upon written notice to the custodial parent at least 30 days in advance of such visitation;

(4) During the odd years, spring break vacation from 9 a.m. Saturday until the following Friday at 6 p.m.;

(5) During the even years, Thanksgiving vacation from Wednesday at 6 p.m. until Sunday at 6 p.m.;

(6) Every other birthday of the child from 6 p.m. on said date until 8 a.m. the following morning;

(7) Every Father/Mother's Day from 9 a.m. until 6 p.m. of the same day;

(8) On the birthday of the mother/father from 3 p.m. on said date until 8 p.m. of the same day;

(9) Any other reasonable times and places upon which the parties can agree; and

(10) Each party shall keep the other informed on a current basis as to the primary residence, address and telephone number where the children reside or visit.

(B) Activities of the minor children. Both the husband and wife desire to be involved in the various activities of their minor children. These include academic, religious, civic (such as Scouts or other civic-related organizations or community projects), cultural (such as music, theater, and the like), athletic, purchase of clothing, and medical and dental activities of the children. The husband and wife agree to cooperate with the other in adjusting their schedules to assure that the children are delivered to and returned from any such activity. It is further agreed and understood that both parties will notify one another of all conferences, programs, or events relating to such activities in such a way that both parties will have an opportunity to participate in such activities of the children.

Should the husband and wife be unable to agree on any aspect of the academic, religious, civic, cultural, athletic, or medical and dental activities of the children, the following party is hereby designated as having the primary authority and responsibility regarding involvement in said activity:

- Academic   Wife   (Can select Husband or Wife)
- Religious   Wife   (Can select Husband or Wife)
- Civic   Husband (Can select Husband or Wife)
- Cultural   Husband (Can select Husband or Wife)
- Athletic   Husband (Can select Husband or Wife)
- Medical/Dental Wife   (Can select Husband or Wife)

The exercise of this primary authority is in no way intended to negate the responsibility of the parties to notify and communicate with each other.

How do You Determine the Primary Custodian?

In a custody dispute, it is important to illustrate to the court that one parent has been the primary custodian of the children during the marriage. This parent usually is the one who receives primary custody of the children after the divorce, unless there are significant conflicting circumstances. To determine who is the primary custodian, you need to determine who performs most of the following activities for the children:

- Who helps the children get dressed for school?
- Who fixes breakfast for the children?
- Who packs the children's lunch for school?
- Who helps the children with their homework?
- Who participates in school activities with the children?
- Who takes care of the children after school?
- Who bathes the children?
- Who takes the children to school?

- Who takes the children to the doctor?
- Who takes the children shopping?
- Who takes the children to religious activities?
- Who arranges for the children's extracurricular activities?
- Who helps the children in various stages of development?

What a Parent Should Know About a Child Before Entering Into a Custody Battle

Before entering into a custody battle, make certain you know answers to basic questions concerning the care of your child. Any parent who has participated in the majority of the activities outlined above should be able to answer most of the following questions without hesitation:

- Who is the child's doctor?
- Where is his office?
- What allergies does the child have?
- Who is the child's dentist?
- Who is the child's principal?
- Who is the child's teacher?
- What is the child's favorite subject in school?
- Who is the child's day care provider?
- How often does the child go to day care?
- Name the child's three best friends.
- What is the child's favorite book?
- What is the child's favorite color?
- What special needs does the child have?
- What size shoe does the child wear?
- What size clothes does the child wear?

Sometimes a parent who means well, but hasn't taken an active role in the child care, needs time to establish a role with the child and learn these things about the child before proceeding with a custody battle. One client who came into our office was convinced his wife was mentally unstable and could not care for their son anymore. Although he had worked long hours and traveled for his company, he was determined to change all of that after the divorce. For months, he strengthened his position with the child and kept a journal of his wife's erratic behavior.

After a particularly disturbing weekend at home, the father alerted us to file the divorce, and he moved the child elsewhere for the child's protection. Because he had prepared so well and could show how his wife's mental state was affecting his son, the man won sole custody of the child and the wife received limited visitation.

Potential Custody/Visitation Problems

"I have always told my son the truth. I think it is important to tell him that his mother is a fat alcoholic." This was the straight-faced declaration of the father of a five-year-old. Doesn't this sound as though the pain of the father will cause visitation problems in the future? I am a firm believer that there are things about the divorce that the children do not need to know.

It is worth noting that if young children are involved in the divorce, it is almost guaranteed there will be visitation problems in the future. No settlement agreement can address all of the potential circumstances that arise in the raising of children. Disputes may involve the simplest of issues, from a parent who cannot pick up the child at a scheduled time due to unforeseen circumstances, to a child who has an important event during a visitation period and the non-custodial parent refuses to take the child to the event. There are divorces without these problems, but these are the exception.

People often call our office in a panic because an ex-spouse was 10 minutes late returning the child from visitation. One domestic judge asked the attorneys involved in a visitation dispute if their clients had lost their minds. In many instances, clients *do* feel they are losing their minds because of all the emotions involved. Why would anyone get the court involved because the ex brought the child back 10 minutes late? Plenty of married couples run late. Yet, when a court order spells out a visitation schedule, parents sometimes believe there are absolutely no exceptions to the rule. Ten minutes may seem like a big deal to that parent. But in the scheme of things, life will go on.

In many instances, parents have not been allowed to take a child to events such as baseball or football games, because the games were not during a visitation period. It is no wonder the two parents ended up divorced, when they are not able to separate their hatred for each other long enough to allow a child to go to a baseball game. Even worse, one parent will tell the child, "Yes, I would like to let you go to the game, but I can't trust your father to bring you home on time." Now, the child has not only been denied an opportunity to be with the other parent. The child has also been placed in the middle of a petty visitation dispute.

Children Deserve Both Parents

"Children spell love 'T-I-M-E'." This is a wonderful quote from John Croyle, founder of the Big Oak Ranch Children's Home.

Children in a divorce deserve an equivalent amount of guidance from both parents. The children did not cause or deserve the divorce, and they are entitled to have two parents who don't use the children as pawns against each other. I am amazed at the number of parents who will say they are always honest with their child, so they tell the child, "your mother was having an affair and she left us for someone else." Say the child is only five years old. He or she is not old enough to understand a divorce. Most of the time, a parent is simply trying to turn the child against the other parent by filling the child's head with negative images.

I will never forget a case I had where a mother talked so badly about the father all week long that when it came time for the week-end visitation, the children didn't want to go with their father. When confronted, the mother said she could not understand why the children would not go. Eventually, it was shown that the mother had said so many negative things about the father that the children truly believed that he was a terrible monster. The mother would give the children a tape recorder to record their father at the front door, since she believed he always lied to them. These children would pick up the phone when their father called and begin recording. Or they would turn the recorder on whenever he came to the door to pick them up. Amazingly though, the father was a wonderful individual and a good father.

When he sued for custody, the children testified that they loved their father very much, but they did not want to hurt their mother's feelings by going with their father. So they just didn't go on the visitation. The mother was found in contempt of court for willfully interfering with a divorce decree and was sentenced to jail. Actually, that mother should have lost custody for the example she set. She not only taught the children to lie, but she also created a barrier that nearly destroyed the father's relationship with the children. If not for the father's persistence, he likely would have had to give up on his children altogether.

The above example illustrates the horrible way children are used as pawns during and after a divorce. These children deserve better. I do everything I can to ensure that people do not use their children in such a manner. There are always differences of opinion over who is the better parent, but those disputes should be between the parents. As a rule, I only put a child on the witness stand when the client and I have made a decision that, due to the overwhelming need for the testimony, we have no other choice.

If the child witnessed a particularly abusive incident, the child's testimony may be required. But lawyers who put a child on the stand merely to ask a five-year-old which parent he or she wants to live with should be ashamed. Even worse for them, it's a strategy most judges detest and often won't forgive. Many times I question whether the parties and their lawyers know the destructive power they hold and the damage they can do to a child by involving them in the divorce.

Perhaps the greatest advice I can offer concerning the issue of custody is that your children will always remember how you handle the divorce. If you neglect them, they will never forget it. If you use them as pawns, they will never forget it nor will they likely ever forgive you. One day they will grow up, and the games their parents played with their lives will become more apparent. Because of that, the only winning course for any parent is to do what is in the best interest of the children. Usually, there is a clear-cut way to address this issue. That is to not involve the children in the divorce. The problem is that most clients may not want to accept the answer. If you truly have your children's best interest at heart, you will always accept the answer, even if it means tremendous personal sacrifice to you. To do otherwise would harm not only your children, but your own self worth.

*How can she possibly need that much
money to support three children? I won't
have any money left for me.
Can't she get a second job?*

Anonymous opposing party

CHAPTER 12

Child Support

In Alabama, child support is calculated by the Child Support Guidelines, which must be followed in all cases involving children under the age of 19. Prior to the passage of the Child Support Guidelines, child support was calculated in a variety of ways, and some judges and parties even waived support in many cases. But the law is clear now that child support must be paid and cannot be waived, even with a parent's consent. Only in limited circumstances will the court even consider a reduction in child support when the non-custodial parent spends extra time with the child, or has travel expenses or high medical costs relating to the child.

The Support Formula

Child support is based on a formula that considers both parents' gross monthly income, that is, their total monthly income prior to any deductions for taxes or other forms of withholding. Under the guidelines, both parents' gross monthly income is totaled. That figure then determines the child support payment on a pro rata basis. The payment increases as the number of children increase. However, it is important to note that the payment does not increase in an equal amount per child. The Child Support Guidelines contain a chart similar to the federal income tax charts, that increases with the income of the parents and the number of children.

The child support calculation also considers day care expenses and health insurance costs related to the children. If the parent paying child support also pays for health insurance, that parent receives a credit against the child support for the payment of that premium.

Appendix B at the end of this book contains an example child support form which assumes the parties have two children, an income of $2,000 a month for the husband and $1,000 for the wife, day care costs of $250 and health insurance costs of $164. There's a blank Child Support Guideline form, as well as the schedule of Basic Child Support obligations under varied levels of combined monthly gross income for the parents. There is also an example of a Child Support Income Affidavit, which must be signed by each parent. The forms will help you estimate the amount of child support that may be applicable in your case, but your lawyer can provide you with exact numbers. There are many variables in the child support calculations, so it is strongly suggested that you seek legal advice concerning the applicability of the Child Support Guidelines to your case.

The Child Support Guidelines contain certain limitations on child care costs. You may be limited to the Department of Human Resources' recommended guidelines for day care expenses. If so, these numbers may be considerably less than the cost of private child care, and the custodial parent may be forced to bear the majority of this expense unless there is a variation in the agreement with the non-custodial parent.

If the parent paying child support is unemployed, he or she may not be required to make payments until he obtains employment, unless the court can calculate income based on earning potential. If a payor parent is self-employed, it may be difficult, if not impossible, to estimate the party's true income. Many self-employed people receive income in cash, and this income is difficult to prove in a contested divorce. If you are involved in a divorce with a self-employed person, financial records and other documentation are extremely important and valuable in proving your case. Sometimes, the lawyer will look at consumption rather than income and illustrate to the court the purchases made by the spouse, despite the declared income.

Income Withholding Orders

Child support can be withheld directly from a spouse's paycheck in Alabama through an Income Withholding Order, providing the payor spouse lives in the state or his employer has a business here. Most jurisdictions require an Income Withholding Order be entered automatically, unless the parties can reach an alternate arrangement whereby the non-custodial spouse pays the custodial spouse directly. These orders are becoming the norm in many cases. They simplify payments and are no longer considered a bad thing in most situations. The Income Withholding Order may be entered in the court clerk's office at the time of the divorce, but not served upon the payor's employer until the payor has become delinquent in his or her child support by more than 30 days. If the payment of child support is a concern, it is much simpler to address this issue at the time of divorce than to attempt to enforce an Income Withholding Order in the future. At the same time, if a spouse has been actively involved in the care of the children, he or she may prefer that the employer not be forced to generate one check for child support and the remainder of his or her income in another check.

Post-Majority College Support

Child support usually must be paid until the children reach the age of majority (19), unless the children marry or become self-supporting. It is possible to receive child support beyond the age of majority for payment of specific college and other education-related expenses. If at all possible, the payment of college expenses should be addressed in the settlement of the divorce. Most settlement agreements specify that one parent will pay these expenses, or that the parties will divide them in some pro rata share. These expenses may include tuition, books, and room and board. Other items such as a weekly allowance, books, fees, fraternity and sorority expenses and transportation to and from school can be agreed to by the parties. But the court will not likely require a parent to pay for these items. The court usually will not require private tuition to be paid without a prior agreement between the parties. If, for example, a child wants to attend a private university, the agreement should specify the anticipated school and/or expenses to avoid any confusion in the future. Vanderbilt or Duke may be the preferred choices. In this case, the other parent may argue that the local community college can also provide a college degree, in an attempt to minimize the parent's obligations. Usually, scholarships will be credited against these expenses. Child support does not continue, however, in addition to the college support. Instead, the custodial parent is usually limited to specific college expenses.

The college obligation usually continues until each child receives his or her undergraduate degree, but no longer than a specified time period from the date he or she graduates from high school. Usually the child must maintain at least an overall "C" average and be on track toward obtaining a college degree within the specified time period, or the parent's obligation shall terminate. In addition, most parents request access to the child's grades and academic standing.

If a parent will not agree to the payment of college expenses at the time of settlement, or if the children have not reached high school at the time of the divorce, the court may not require college to be addressed. In that event, it is possible to reserve the issue of college support in the settlement agreement. This gives the custodial parent the right to come back to court to ask for the payment of these expenses in the future. A formal request must be made to the court before the child reaches the age of 19, or it is forever waived. If this is a contested issue, the court will look to the actual expenses of the college education and the child's scholastic aptitude for college. Rarely will the court force a parent to pay for college for a student who does poorly in school. And you must realize that when the issue of college support is reserved, it will be difficult to plan for this major expense in the future and additional attorney's fees will be required to implement the request.

I was confounded by the woman who, at the close of the case, asked me why I would not make her unemployed, alcoholic husband get a job. I said to her, "How can you expect me to do in one trial what you couldn't accomplish in 20 years?"

An Alabama Circuit Court Judge

CHAPTER 13

Domestic Violence: The Veil is Lifted

According to statistics provided by the National Coalition Against Domestic Violence, 20,000 homicides occur annually across the country due to domestic violence. Shockingly, domestic violence is the number one cause of injury to women in this country — more than automobile accidents, rapes and muggings combined. For this reason alone, divorce may provide an outlet for victims of domestic violence to escape the violence by leaving the marriage. If you are a victim of domestic violence, you should immediately seek help to protect yourself and your children.

It is important to recognize the numerous sources of support to victims of domestic violence. Getting help requires you to take the most difficult step initially and admit that you are in an abusive relationship. If your spouse does any of the following things, you may need to seek professional help immediately.

Signs of Physical Abuse

Does your spouse hit, kick or strike you?
Does your spouse threaten you with guns or other weapons?

Does your spouse scream at you or threaten you?

Does your spouse break items throughout the house?

Does your spouse force sex?

Does your spouse threaten to harm you if you leave?

If any of the above things are happening in your relationship, you may need to take immediate action to protect yourself. This means you need to get professional help to explain your options. If you are in a truly dangerous situation, you need to leave that situation. If necessary, stay with other family members, friends or in a shelter until you can obtain relief through the court. If you have to leave due to an abusive situation, make every effort to take your children with you. If this is an issue in your case, seek legal help before taking further action.

Involving the Police

If the situation warrants, call the police if you are being threatened. The police can immediately intervene to help address the situation. If you cannot call the police before you leave, simply call them from a safe location. If the police believe sufficient evidence exists, they can arrest your spouse on the scene. The police may, however, ask you to swear out a warrant pressing charges against the spouse. This process usually involves you swearing out a warrant with a magistrate in the jurisdiction where the abuse occurred. Once the warrant has been issued, the police will arrest the spouse and the case will be set for trial. Please be aware, however, that this is a very lengthy and involved process. If it is a first offense, the court may recommend counselling rather than jail time. The sooner you start to establish a history of this type of behavior, the more likely the court will put that spouse in jail for repeated incidents.

Keep in mind that statistics show a woman is abused in the U.S. every 15 seconds. If you are in this type of situation, you need to seek help immediately, before the situation escalates to a potentially fatal situation. This is perhaps the great lesson learned by the O.J. Simpson case. Now people are much more aware of the possibility for domestic violence after having followed this case.

When A Child is Abused

The most emotional type of case we deal with involves child abuse — and more specifically — sexual abuse. This type of case usually involves a young child that has been physically or sexually abused by a parent or close family member or friend. We have a policy in our office that we will not represent a parent who has admitted or been shown to have abused their child. I do not want to participate in this type of case unless I am on the side of the parent protecting the child. These cases require immediate action and usually involve facts that increase in severity as the case proceeds and more information becomes available. Do not make the mistake of thinking that this type of abuse cannot happen to your child. Remember that child abuse of any kind can occur in any type of racial, ethnic, religious or economic group. We have represented parents from all types of economic and social backgrounds, and I firmly believe that child abuse can occur in even the wealthiest of families. They simply have the resources to cover up abuse more readily.

Fraudulent Allegations

It is important to note, however, that spousal abuse and child abuse is often brought up fraudulently by the opposing party in an attempt to affect the outcome of the case. It is very discouraging to see parents lie about physical or sexual abuse immediately after a divorce complaint has been filed. It amazes me that the parent never took any action about those concerns until the other spouse filed for divorce. Now great effort is given to keep the abusive spouse away from the children. Why did that spouse never file for divorce or even complain to the police or the doctor about the abuse? Sadly, so many parents have lied about this type of abuse that they have created a much higher burden for the legitimate abuse cases to meet to show the abuse because there is such a presumption that the other spouse is lying.

The Department of Human Resources usually investigates when neglect or child abuse is reported to the agency. The major source of child abuse or neglect reports come from schools followed by law enforcement agencies, relatives, parents, social agencies, neighbors, hospitals, mental health employees and physicians. If the Department of Human Resources believes the child is in danger, it has the power to remove the child from the home immediately. The Department's goal, however, is to keep the child with one of the parents rather than remove the child from the home and the agency will make every effort to keep the child with a family member.

It is very disturbing to report that three children die every day from child abuse and neglect in the United States and 483 children are seriously harmed or disabled every day as a result of abuse and neglect, according to the Exchange Club of Birmingham. Child abuse victims can eventually overcome the scars of their abuse, but this may require extensive counselling and concentrated efforts on the parent's behalf.

Documenting Abuse

If you believe that your child may be the victim of child abuse, it is imperative that you document the abuse with sound medical evidence, including doctor's reports and photographs. There is no piece of evidence more damaging than a photograph of the bruised face of a child during a divorce trial. Immediately seek professional legal and medical help in order to ensure your child receives the necessary protection he or she deserves. Your pediatrician is a great source of immediate help and can direct you to other professional help. Please be aware, however, that if the professional believes that child abuse is indicated, he or she has a duty to report the abuse to the appropriate agency and that agency will act accordingly. Therefore, you need to be aware that you may be starting an action that you cannot stop once you seek professional help. You need to have made all of the necessary preparations to deal with it, including seeking sound legal advice concerning the divorce.

*But in this world nothing can
be said to be certain,
except death and taxes.*

Benjamin Franklin

CHAPTER 14

Easily Overlooked:
Income Taxes and Insurance

Divorcing couples must address the issue of income tax liability in the settlement agreement. The parties may or may not be able to file joint or individual returns for the year of the divorce, depending on their particular situation and the timing of the divorce. It is strongly suggested that you consult with your accountant as to the applicability of any tax consequences related to your divorce. If you do not have an accountant, your lawyer can suggest one who can quickly evaluate the impact of your agreement from a tax standpoint. In addition, the issues related to dividing any liability or refund for the year must also be addressed in the settlement agreement.

Tax Liability

The previous year's tax liabilities or refund may need to be considered in the settlement agreement. Language should be added that specifies who is responsible for any deficiency assessment for liabilities for the prior tax year. Many spouses are not aware of the information contained in the tax returns, and are usually very surprised if a deficiency or audit arises after the divorce.

95

Who receives the tax exemptions for the children is an important element of the settlement agreement. Generally, the custodial parent is awarded the income tax exemptions for any children, since the Child Support Guidelines are based on the custodial parent receiving the exemptions. However, the parties may agree to divide or split the exemptions, due to other factors related to the settlement. For example, if one spouse is not working and has little income, tax exemptions may not help that spouse. Likewise, the exemptions may benefit a spouse at a higher income much more than it might the spouse who is working for a minimal income.

An Internal Revenue Service form usually is required to claim the children as an exemption after the divorce. This form may need to be executed in order to satisfy the Internal Revenue Service concerning the exemptions in the future. You should consult with your lawyer and accountant in more detail concerning these issues in order to protect your interests.

Health Insurance for the Children

One parent usually is required to provide and maintain hospital and major medical insurance for a minor child until that child reaches age 19. If a child attends college, the coverage may be continued by agreement until the child graduates. If there is no health insurance coverage available to either spouse, it may be difficult to force a party to obtain coverage. Accordingly, if a spouse is unemployed, benefits such as health insurance may also be difficult to obtain after the divorce.

The settlement agreement should address which party will be responsible for any medical expenses not covered by the health insurance. Traditionally, either one spouse is fully responsible for these expenses, or the parties agree to equally split these amounts. These expenses include reasonable charges for doctor, hospital, medical, prescription drug, optical, dental, orthodontic, or other medically-related expenses. This issue should not be taken lightly, because medical expenses associated with children can be monumental. In addition, if a child is diagnosed with a major illness such as leukemia, these expenses can be devastating and lead to bankruptcy.

Health Insurance for the Spouse

Health insurance for a divorcing spouse can be a major issue in the settlement of a case. Generally, most health insurance plans will not allow a spouse to continue to provide coverage for his or her ex. Therefore, a spouse needing coverage has several options. First, a spouse may obtain coverage through an employer. This often is the cheapest solution to this problem.

Another option: the spouse may continue health insurance coverage through the other spouse's insurance plan under the COBRA plan for a limited time. COBRA is a federal law that provides, among other things, the opportunity for a former spouse to continue coverage for a specific period of time. The premiums associated with COBRA coverage are often considerably higher than the previous payments through the employer. Each spouse should confirm that this type of coverage is available before the final resolution of the case. The settlement agreement should also address who pays the premiums for this coverage.

Finally, the spouse can obtain coverage through an independent source. The settlement agreement can specify that the other spouse must pay the premiums for a specified period of time. However, this is a difficult provision to obtain in a divorce, and it may be extremely difficult to be successful at trial with such a request.

Importantly, pre-existing conditions may not be covered under the new insurance. Therefore, if one spouse has a major health condition such as cancer or a heart condition, the condition may not be covered by the new insurance after the divorce. If this is a possibility, this issue should be very closely examined in order to assess the costs associated with medical care after the divorce. Many medical conditions such as cancer and other major illnesses can play a large role in a party's need for alimony due to the costs associated with the illness, as well as the limitations the illness may place on the spouse's ability to work. As a result, health conditions may be a very disputed issue in your divorce, due to the potential implications. For example, the husband of an ill wife may argue that she is not really sick, but simply making up an illness to get sympathy. To refute this claim, the wife's attorney may have to get a physician to testify to the wife's condition and its impact on her ability to work. Getting a doctor to testify in court is an expensive proposition. However, there may be a large amount of money at stake that would make such an investment worthwhile. The client may significantly reduce the cost by getting all medical records related to the condition for the lawyer to review. Otherwise, the lawyer will likely have to subpoena the medical records at considerable expense.

Life Insurance

If there are children involved and child support and other expenses are addressed in the settlement agreement, life insurance should be considered in the event the payor spouse dies. Likewise, if alimony or other financial payments are being made to the other spouse, the payor spouse should be required to maintain adequate insurance until there is no longer an obligation. It is a common practice that the payor spouse be required to maintain specific life insurance policies and name the spouse or children as beneficiaries while he or she has a financial obligation under the divorce. The settlement agreement should specify that the payor spouse must provide life insurance coverage on his life of not less than a specified dollar amount, for a certain time period. The children or the ex-spouse should be the beneficiary of this insurance.

The settlement agreement should specify that the obligated

spouse not modify the life insurance policies or diminish the value of the life insurance in any way, either by loan, pledge, assignment or reduction. Often, if children are involved, one spouse may require a trust be established for the life insurance proceeds. Under such a trust, the payor spouse specifies a trustee — often the former spouse or family member — who is required to use the life insurance proceeds for the benefit of each child. When the child reaches a specified age, such as 21, the trustee is usually required to distribute the entire remaining proceeds to the child.

The next time I think about getting married, instead I'll just find a woman who hates me and buy her a house.

Lewis Grizzard

CHAPTER 15

Who Gets the House?

How many people live in a home they cannot afford? Lending institution practices allow people to borrow the maximum amount of money that they, as a couple, can just barely afford to pay back. The crisis occurs when divorce takes place and these people are trying to provide for two separate households along with child support payments after the divorce.

Do You Really Want It?

Clients often believe they "have to keep the house." But after the divorce, they often find they no longer want to live there because of bad memories. Whether they want to keep the house, of course, is irrelevant if they cannot make the payments. With all of these issues at hand, the marital residence is often one of the biggest concerns in a property settlement.

A good matrimonial law attorney will examine the client's financial ability to maintain the residence before recommending how to handle the residence. This generally involves looking at the income of the client and any potential child support or alimony payments, coupled with the debts for which that party will be responsible. The budget form included in Appendix A will prove very beneficial in determining whether or not you can afford to keep the residence. This may lead to a stark realization about the consequences of the divorce, but it is much better to realize ahead of time that you cannot afford the house, than to fight for two years to get a house that you cannot afford.

Once you determine whether to keep the residence, several options are available which include the following:

- Sell the Home and Divide the Equity
- Transfer the Home to the Other Spouse
- Transfer the Home to the Other Spouse For a Certain Number of Years and Then Sell it
- Deed the Home to One Side With a Cash Payment for the Equity

Sell the Home and Divide the Equity

If the parties decide to sell the residence immediately, the settlement agreement should state that it will be sold with the proceeds divided as the parties have agreed. One party may receive all of the equity or the parties may divide it in some way. The property should be appraised and placed on the market for the appraisal amount. In the event the husband and wife cannot agree upon an appraised value, each of them have the right to select an independent appraiser to value the property. These two independent appraisers should then select a third appraiser who will agree on the value of the residence.

The parties should agree on an agent to sell the home. If they cannot agree on an agent, each party will select an agent who will confer and choose a third person to serve as the agent for both parties. Until the real estate sells, the agreement also should specify who pays the mortgage payment, taxes, insurance, and utilities. In addition, the agreement should specify that the party living in the home provide routine maintenance and upkeep. The responsibility for paying the cost of reasonable and necessary repairs, such as structural, heating, cooling, roofing, and the like, also must be addressed.

The cost of necessary repairs or improvements to prepare the house for sale should be deducted from money received for the real estate, unless one of the parties agrees to bear this cost.

The agreement should also specify that when the house is sold, the following items will be deducted from the gross sales price:

- The amount of the mortgage;
- The brokerage commission;
- Legal fees related to the sale;
- Cost of repairs or improvements;
- Cost of sale;
- Any other related terms of the settlement agreement, such as the payment of another debt.

Transfer the Home
To the Other Spouse

If one party merely transfers his or her interest to the other party, the agreement should specify that the transferring party conveys all of their interest in the residence and that they agree to execute a warranty or quit claim deed as part of the settlement agreement. The agreement should also specify who shall be solely responsible for the mortgage indebtedness on the residence.

Impact of Keeping the Existing Mortgage

If it was a joint debt, both parties will remain on the mortgage obligation, unless the property is refinanced. As a result, if the responsible party defaults on the mortgage, the mortgage company may look to the party that transferred their interest for payment of the debt. Likewise, this mortgage obligation will show up on a credit report and will have to be addressed in future loan applications. This can sometimes be handled by showing the creditor a copy of the divorce decree that indicates the other spouse is responsible for the mortgage obligation. If that spouse has not paid the obligation, though, it can cause tremendous hardship and difficulties for the other spouse. It may require court action to either enforce payment of the mortgage or to force the sale of the residence. In many cases, this problem cannot be avoided because the other spouse cannot qualify for the mortgage alone.

Transfer the Home to the Other Spouse For a Certain Number of Years and Then Sell It

It is also possible to specify in the settlement agreement that one party shall have sole use of the home for a specified period of time, and then it will be sold with the equity divided in a specified fashion. This option is common when there are young children and the immediate sale of the residence would be disruptive to their lives. Sometimes the wife is awarded the property for several months or years — until the children turn 19, complete college or move out on their own — or until the wife remarries.

The settlement agreement must address the period of time for which the spouse has use of the residence and what events are necessary to trigger a sale. The agreement must also consider who should provide routine maintenance and upkeep, as well as payment of the mortgage obligation. If the spouse gets the home for a long period of time, the parties must address whether the equity to be divided shall be capped at its present value — and what that value might be — or at the future value at the time of sale. Obviously, if one spouse makes all of the payments after the divorce, they will not likely want to share the appreciation in the residence with their former spouse.

Deed the Home to One Side
With A Cash Payment for the Equity

Under this option, one party pays the other party a specified sum in consideration of receiving the marital residence. The terms of the payment of this sum must be addressed in the settlement agreement, along with the payment of the mortgage obligation. In addition, the issues discussed above related to the existing mortgage indebtedness must also be addressed.

Tax Consequences From the Sale of the Home

There may be tax consequences associated with the sale of the family home that may greatly affect the value of the award. For example, there may be capital gains taxes associated with the appreciation in equity in the residence over the original purchase price. In addition, there are specific time limits in which you must transfer the equity to a new residence in order to avoid additional tax consequences. You may want to consider meeting with your accountant to analyze any potential tax liabilities associated with the residence before making a final determination.

People often want to know why I'm not as good as Solomon. I remind them that I'm only a judge. Solomon got to be king. If I was also a king, I could make some changes!

An Alabama Circuit Court Judge

CHAPTER 16

The Dealbreaker:
Who Gets the Toaster Oven

For some people, custody of their children is the most important, hotly contested issue in a divorce. For others, who gets the Ming Dynasty vase given as a wedding present or the Elvis Presley records that belonged to them before the marriage are the hot topics.

Assets Worth the Fight

The property at issue usually consists of that which each spouse brought into the marriage, marital property acquired by both spouses during the marriage, gifts and inheritances received by both spouses during the marriage, and separate property purchased by both spouses during the marriage. A multitude of potential assets will need to be addressed in the settlement agreement. In addition, any liabilities associated with these assets must also be addressed.

These assets may include the following:

- Furniture and furnishings of the residence
- Bank accounts
- Stocks
- Bonds

- Checking accounts
- Savings accounts
- Life insurance
- Retirement plans
- Individual retirement accounts
- 401K plans
- Jewelry
- Automobiles
- Antiques
- Family heirlooms
- Sporting equipment
- Artworks
- China, silver, crystal
- Boats and trailers
- Personal collections such as coins and stamps
- Gun collections
- Business equipment
- Tools
- Yard equipment
- Whatever asset your spouse treasures

In an ideal situation, both spouses will be able to agree on most, if not all, of the property division. In that event, the settlement agreement needs to address the specific division of property and the responsibility of each party for any debts.

Factors The Court Considers

If the parties cannot agree on a division of the property, the court will look to a wide variety of factors in the division of the property, including the following:
- Ownership of the property
- If the property was owned prior to the marriage

- If the property was purchased during the marriage
- Any contributions to the property by either party, including money and labor
- Length of the marriage
- The parties' respective ages, health, occupations, employability and ability to be trained
- The degree to which a spouse has diminished his or her future earning capacity because of years spent caring for the children
- The opportunity for each spouse to acquire additional capital, assets or income in the future
- What alimony payments will be made
- What each party should equitably receive in the division
- The fault of the parties

You Should Decide

It is in the parties' best interest to work out an amicable division of the personal property, instead of having a judge do it. For one thing, the parties are a lot more in tune to what they really want. Secondly, the parties have a lot more time available to go into painstaking detail. A judge, on the other hand, doesn't really want to divide personal property. He will deal with the property division much more quickly, as part of the resolution of the entire case. He doesn't have the time to ruminate over the fact that you are fond of that armoire in the bedroom, or that only you watched the big-screen television.

"Unless there was no other way, I would not want to have a judge decide property and custody issues," says one Alabama Circuit Court judge. "Our knowledge of the history and facts of the case is simply too limited. For that reason, I have become a strong advocate of mediation, where the parties can take more time to expand upon a solution than the judge can in a trial setting."

Often the judge will draw a big line somewhere down the list of property. He may split the property evenly, but he may also split the property very unevenly. If one party does not get a particular piece of property, it may be gone forever if the other spouse does not want to trade it for something else. In summary, even if you have to go to trial over more significant issues, try your best to work out the personal property issues with your spouse prior to trial.

Don't get caught up in an ego war over personal property so that when all the dust settles, you have paid your lawyer thousands of dollars to get hundreds of dollars worth of stuff. For example, I remember a horrible custody battle that we tried in court for several days and then nearly resolved, except the settlement talks failed over possession of a Lincoln Towncar. Keep in mind, the custody issue was resolved, but we could not settle the issues concerning this automobile. When that type of situation happens, the parties' true priorities become very clear. Unfortunately, in this case, the car proved to be far more important to the parties than the children. No wonder the parties were getting a divorce!

The following chapter addresses how several of the major personal property issues can be addressed in a settlement agreement. Any of these issues may turn out to be the simplest or the biggest issue in your divorce, depending on the actual facts of your case.

A big case is never simple;
neither is a small one.

Anonymous Divorce Lawyer

CHAPTER 17

Dividing Major
Assets of the Marriage

The following discussion addresses how several of the major personal property division issues can be handled in a settlement agreement. Please note, however, that in the division of marital property, no one rule will not apply in every case, and the overall settlement will be weighed as a whole. All of these assets have a value, as does an award of alimony or a lump sum settlement payment. Therefore, it is impossible to address one issue individually, and in fact, the complete property settlement usually must be addressed as a whole.

Personal Property

Several avenues are available for handling the division of personal property. This section generally applies to the household furniture and furnishings, goods, wares and appliances, along with each individual's clothing, jewelry and personal items. Typically, most settlement agreements either specify that the parties have already divided the personal property and that neither party makes any claim to the other's property, or the agreement will contain a specific list of the property each party is to receive. This may or may not be an important issue to address in the settlement agreement. If the spouses are fairly amicable, they may be able to divide the household property on their own. However, it may be impossible for the parties to agree on the simplest of issues, such as the division of towels and sheets. If so, the agreement needs to specify every item each party receives. If the agreement states that the wife shall receive one-half of the pictures in the residence, it needs to specify exactly what pictures. Likewise, you may own assets in an odd number that cannot be divided. You may spend considerably more on legal fees to fight over a toaster or a couch than you would spend replacing that item. Therefore, every client must assess whether the emotional and financial cost of fighting over certain property is worth the end result. Many clients later claim that their decisions were based more on ego and pride than logic and that they did not even want the asset after they received it, due to the memories associated with fighting over it.

Closely-Held Businesses

If a business is involved in the divorce, the agreement needs to specify who shall receive the business and how the business will be managed after the divorce. If one party is to receive the business, the agreement needs to specify if the other spouse is obligated for any debts or taxes of the business. It also needs to specify who will pay any future debts and taxes associated with the business. In addition, if the business is successful, it may be wise to have an independent accounting of the books and records of the business to determine its true value before finalizing the settlement.

It is almost comical the manner in which businesses seem to be worth so much less to the party running the business during the pendency of a divorce. For example, most business owners claim the last three years were the best years ever for the business, and the business is now likely to suffer a significant decrease in income. Further, these same owners will claim that the market is way off and their sales are suffering. Ironically, history also indicates that these same businesses also seem to begin to prosper again right after the divorce. Businesses should be reviewed very closely due to the potential for the owners to drastically affect the income figures during the divorce.

I recall one business owner who had a very successful business at issue in a hotly contested case. The owner claimed the business was only worth $20,000 or less. We knew during the trial that the business was worth many times more than that. Upon hearing the ridiculous quote on the value, we immediately offered to purchase the business for $40,000 and guaranteed we could have a cashier's check to him within three hours. Amazingly, the owner would not sell the business even at twice the previously stated value because "there are a lot of factors that go into valuing a business and he felt its potential was there." Of course, that was true and he knew it, since he had been practicing creative accounting. Once the owner refused to take the bait at twice the claimed value of the business, we immediately began concentrating on the value of the business and proved its true value to be much higher. As a result, the overall settlement was drastically affected when the business turned out to be worth much more money.

Retirement Accounts

A spouse may be entitled, in certain cases, to a share of the other spouse's retirement plan in a property division. This is a complex issue of the law that must be addressed appropriately. Likewise, retirement benefits may be one of the largest marital assets of the parties, and should be considered before any determination is made on the fairness of the overall settlement agreement. In many long term marriages, the husband may have a retirement plan valued several times more than the equity in the marital residence. A spouse may be making a mistake if she accepts the marital residence in lieu of a share of the husband's retirement plan. If this is applicable, clients should make every effort to obtain a recent statement for the retirement plan, evidencing its present value as well as a valuation of the plan. If this data is not readily available, a lawyer can obtain the information from the account manager through the discovery process.

In addition, the survivor benefits under the retirement plan that are applicable in the event of the spouse's death may also provide security for a spouse and should be addressed in the settlement agreement. Lastly, it is important that the settlement agreement state that any benefits payable under the agreement cannot be assigned or reduced in any fashion. If this is an issue in your divorce, it may be wise to spend some time verifying the actual values of the retirement plan and tax complications with your lawyer and your accountant.

Your lawyer needs to be well versed in the changes in the law concerning retirement plans and the use of a Qualified Domestic Relations Order (QDRO) to divide the plan. Under a QDRO, the plan is basically split into two separate plans to minimize the tax liability that may be associated with dividing the plan prior to maturity.

A marriage isn't a financial investment for which someone else is responsible. If it goes sour, don't expect to get your money back.

An Alabama Circuit Court Judge

CHAPTER 18

Alimony

A general rule applies to any discussion of alimony in a divorce: those wanting alimony think it is fair, and those paying alimony think it is a form of cruel and unusual punishment. There are limited circumstances where a spouse is willing to pay a reasonable amount of alimony, but those cases are the exception and not the rule. There is usually considerable debate as to the amount and length of the term of the alimony payment. The following discussion summarizes the basic forms of alimony and the factors the court considers in making an award of alimony.

Rehabilitative Alimony

This form of alimony is designed to be for a short term, to help a spouse recover financially after the divorce. Rehabilitative alimony is appropriate if the wife has not worked in several years, or if she is working but needs time to recover from the financial impact of the divorce. The goal of rehabilitative alimony is to rehabilitate the spouse over time and not to support her indefinitely.

Alimony in Gross

Another option consists of one spouse paying a lump sum to the other spouse as part of the property settlement. This payment is usually characterized as alimony in gross, and the settlement agreement should specify the amount and terms of the payment. Certain forms of alimony in gross may be dischargeable in bankruptcy, and any provisions in this area should be closely examined with your lawyer. Alimony in gross cannot be modified, even if circumstances change.

Periodic Alimony

Periodic alimony generally is awarded in longer-term marriages (more than 10 years) until the spouse remarries, dies or cohabitates with another individual. However, numerous other factors are considered by a court in making a periodic alimony award. This type of alimony also may be awarded in some short-term marriages.

There are also many misconceptions concerning periodic alimony. For example, most clients believe they are entitled to receive periodic alimony regardless of the length of the marriage, the parties' financial resources or the fault of the parties. The parties' financial resources may be the greatest determining factor in whether periodic alimony is awarded.

If the debts and obligations of the parties leave a negative cash flow, it will be difficult for the court to award a substantial amount of money, despite the needs of a spouse. At the same time, the court may award considerable periodic alimony in long- and short-term marriages where fault on the part of the payor spouse is shown to be responsible for the breakup of the marriage. In those cases, the value of the alimony award may be from several hundred thousand dollars to several million dollars when the payments are valued over the life of the client. Because of these extreme financial ramifications, most paying spouses try to do everything possible to avoid an award of periodic alimony, while most receiving spouses usually do everything possible to ensure such an award.

Periodic alimony can be modified in the future in certain circumstances. The receiving spouse can request a modification if the needs of that party increase or the resources of the paying party increase in the future. The modification issue can provide a tremendous safety net for the receiving spouse, but also provides a tremendous trap for the paying spouse.

You may believe your specified period for paying periodic alimony is over, only to discover your ex-spouse has asked for an extension. Recently, I represented a man who was shocked to learn that his ex-wife filed a petition to extend the alimony he had been paying for 10 years. In the original divorce, the husband gave the wife all of the assets in consideration for paying alimony for only 10 years. The wife had requested five years, but the husband extended it to make sure she had more than enough time to get on her feet. During the 10-year period, the husband's income drastically decreased due to changes in the economy, but he continued to make the large alimony payments at considerable personal sacrifice to him. With one month remaining, his former wife filed a petition to extend the alimony, alleging she still needed the money. After a lengthy court battle, he eventually succeeded in denying her effort to extend the alimony. Whether the alimony can be modified rests largely with the specific language in the agreement and the facts and circumstances of each case. Therefore, the issue of any future modification of the alimony award must be addressed in the settlement agreement. It must be stated that the parties do not intend for it to be modifiable in order to limit the risks at a later date. The language may not be able to guarantee the terms can't be modified, but it certainly will work against a modification.

Periodic alimony is taxable to the receiving spouse and deductible to the paying spouse. Therefore, it may be wise to meet with your accountant to determine the tax consequences of any periodic alimony award before you can properly evaluate the true value of the payment.

Factors Considered by the Court
In Making an Award of Alimony

Numerous factors are considered by the court in determining an appropriate alimony award. A case-by-case analysis in conjunction with the overall property division under the settlement agreement should be determined. The court normally considers the following factors in making an alimony award:

- The apportionment of property under the settlement agreement
- The parties' financial resources
- The length of the marriage
- The respective age, health, occupation, employability, and trainability of the parties
- The degree to which one spouse has diminished his or her future earning capacity or education because of years spent caring for children or serving as a homemaker
- Standard of living during the marriage
- Tax consequences of the awarding of alimony
- The fault of the parties

Tax and Bankruptcy Consequences
Of Alimony

Alimony payments have specific tax consequences in a divorce. The type of alimony a party receives dictates the applicable tax consequences. In general terms, rehabilitative alimony in gross is non-taxable to the receiving spouse and non-deductible to the paying spouse. Periodic alimony, however, is taxable to the receiving spouse and deductible to the paying spouse. These tax consequences may have a significant effect on the actual value of the award and the cost of the award to the paying spouse. Accordingly, divorcing couples should consult with their accountants in conjunction with their attorneys when evaluating the options related to alimony.

In addition, the bankruptcy laws have specific applications for alimony payments. Certain forms of alimony in gross may be dischargeable in a future bankruptcy action, and the issue of dischargeability must be addressed in the settlement agreement. Periodic alimony, on the other hand, is generally not dischargeable in bankruptcy. If you think the other spouse may file bankruptcy, inform your attorney because the terms of the settlement agreement may drastically affect your rights under that bankruptcy.

For example, your spouse may attempt to discharge a large amount of past due alimony payments. Periodic alimony would not normally be dischargeable in bankruptcy while alimony in gross could be dischargeable. To further protect yourself, the original settlement agreement also may need to provide some security, such as a lien against a piece of property, to limit the payor's ability to bankrupt the debt.

*Fairness occurs only when you divide all
the property among the parties
and throw the debts into the sea.*

Anonymous

CHAPTER 19

Apportioning the Debts

Payment of the debts of the parties must be addressed in the settlement agreement, or this issue may come back to haunt one spouse or the other for years to come. The agreement should specify in detail exactly which debts each party is responsible for after the divorce. For each of the debts, the responsible party should indemnify the other from any additional expense incurred resulting from the indebtedness, including an attorney's fee for the enforcement of the indemnification.

Which Debts?

Perhaps the best example of the need to be specific is illustrated by one of the worst agreements I ever saw. It was agreed to several years ago. The agreement (which I had no role in drafting) stated that "the parties have certain debts and the wife shall pay two of the debts and the husband shall pay two of the debts." Only it didn't specify which two debts each party was supposed to pay! As a result of the ambiguity, this type of agreement is very difficult to enforce, because there is no way the court can interpret the specific debts from the vague terms.

Who's Liable?

An individual creditor may still hold a spouse liable in the event the responsible party does not pay a debt for which the other spouse is still a party. But if the responsible party does not make the payments as ordered, the other spouse can take him or her to court on a contempt action. The creditor will still seek payment of the obligation. Therefore, it is wise to pay off as many debts as possible, cancel the accounts or convert them into the name of one spouse. In addition, it may be appropriate for the settlement agreement to specify that certain debts be refinanced within a specific time period to remove the spouse from any obligation.

It is also worth noting that the court does not look favorably upon a spouse who makes a large number of charges on joint credit cards immediately before separating for divorce. As a result, any recent charges need to be substantiated with receipts as being reasonable and appropriate.

Factors Considered in Apportioning Debts

In addressing the responsibility for the marital debts, the court will consider a variety of factors. These factors include the following:
- Whose name the debt is in
- The purpose of the debt
- Who is retaining the asset related to the debt
- Financial resources of the parties
- Any agreement between the parties concerning the debts
- The overall apportionment of property under the settlement agreement
- The length of the marriage
- The fault of the parties

It is helpful for clients to provide their attorneys with a list of all of the debts of the marriage, including a breakdown of debts incurred by the husband, the wife, or jointly. In addition, clients should provide a detailed list of purchases made to account for the debts, and the current status of those assets. This information should also include the name and address of the creditors, as well as the account numbers. Please refer to the exhibit section at the end of this book for summary forms that will help you compile the necessary information concerning the debts and assets of the marriage.

*O'er lawyers fingers, who straight
dream on fees;*

Shakespeare

CHAPTER 20

Attorney's Fees

As stated earlier, you may or may not have to pay your attorney's fees, depending on the facts of the case. Any settlement agreement needs to address who is responsible for payment of the attorney's fees. Typically, it will either state that each party pay their own attorney's fees, or that one party shall pay all or part of the other party's attorney's fees up to a specified amount, or that the fees shall be equally divided between the parties. In a contested divorce, an award of attorney's fees by the court is discretionary, and depends upon the overall terms of the property settlement.

Usually Each Client Pays

Most fee agreements place the ultimate responsibility for payment of the fees with the client. In the event that fees are not awarded by the court or the opposing spouse does not pay the awarded fees, the attorney will likely seek payment of the fees from his or her client. The court may only award a portion of the fees to the client, leaving a balance owed by the client. This court award is usually based upon the overall property award made by the court and not on the court's opinion as to the value of services rendered.

Fees: Good Bargaining Chip

As a strategy, you may want to consider that few people are willing to pay the other spouse's attorney's fee. Let's face it: your attorney has been the source of considerable misery for your spouse. The attorney's fees merely constitute a financial value, as does a bank account or other asset in the divorce. You might agree to pay your own attorney's fees in order to get a larger share of a bank account or asset. A spouse may be willing to give you a $20,000 bank account, for instance, but not $5,000 in attorney's fees, due to ego and pride. Obviously, you would be better served to take the bank account and pay your own attorney's fees.

Justice? You get it in the next world. In this world, you have the law.

William Gaddis, from "A FROLIC OF HIS OWN"

CHAPTER 21

The Miscellany of Divorce

Changing the Wife's Name

Many wives want to return to their maiden name after a divorce. If so, the settlement agreement should specify that the wife may reclaim her former name. This is not critical and can be done at a later date, but will require the completion of additional legal forms. It is simpler to handle this at the time of the divorce by simply requesting the use of a former name in the settlement agreement. However, if there are still young children, many wives do not change their names in an effort to avoid confusion, and some judges refuse to grant the name change for the benefit of the children.

Warranties

The settlement agreement also should specify that both parties agree and stipulate that the agreement makes fair and equitable provisions for the distribution of their property, and that both parties have full knowledge of and have made full disclosure of all separate marital assets. The agreement should specify that both parties are voluntarily executing the agreement and are free of any undue influence or duress other than the normal stresses of divorce.

The agreement should specify that the settlement contains the entire understanding and agreement between the parties, that it is a full and complete settlement, and that there are no representations, warranties, covenants or undertakings other than those expressly set forth in the agreement.

In addition, the agreement should specify that any obligations cannot be discharged under the Bankruptcy Code. While this provision may not fully exempt certain obligations in the bankruptcy court, it may help the party attempting to enforce the obligation in divorce court because it shows the intent of the parties.

Necessary Documents

The settlement agreement should specify that each party will execute and deliver any and all documents that may be necessary to give full effect to the agreement. For example, there may be certain documents, such as car titles or insurance forms, that need to be signed well after the divorce is finalized. Such a provision should be part of everyday common sense. The parties should be able to agree on signing basic documents. However, with the emotions present during and after a divorce, I have found that if it is not specified in the agreement, many parties will argue they do not have to do it. Of course, the agreement does not specify basic premises such as the fact that you are supposed to feed your children, but it is understood that you should. Naturally, however, even basic points such as feeding your children can be disputed by certain types of argumentative spouses simply for the sport of arguing.

Non-Compliance

The agreement should specify that should either party incur any expense or legal fees as a result of the breach of any portion of the settlement agreement by the other party, the court shall award reasonable attorney's fees to the non-defaulting party. While this provision may not be enforceable in every instance, it usually provides considerable leverage to the party attempting to enforce a provision of the agreement in the future.

Modification

It should be specified that any modification or waiver of any provision of the settlement agreement will only be effective if made in writing, executed with the same formality of the settlement agreement and approved by the court. This is important because often a party will claim that "she told me it was okay not to pay the child support."

*Litigation is a machine which you
go into as a pig
and come out as a sausage.*

Ambrose Bierce

CHAPTER 22

Preparing for Trial

For many people, a divorce is the only experience they will ever have in a courthouse. Besides adding to the stress related to going through a divorce, the courthouse provides a very sobering experience for many people. I would highly recommend that anyone going through a litigated divorce go to the courthouse to watch a trial before having to attend your own hearing. It is unsettling for many clients who arrive at a crowded courthouse on the day of a hearing to adjust to the legal process during their own hearing. Your lawyer should be able to direct you to the appropriate courthouse, so that you can view a similar hearing. It is helpful to view your particular judge's demeanor, as well as the process itself. Furthermore, simply to know where the courthouse is located and where the restrooms and vending machines are in the building will make your experience a little easier.

When you go to the courthouse, take a pen and paper so that you can write down any questions you have for your lawyer. You may hear the judge make a statement to one of the other lawyers that you think is directly relevant to your case. You will need to review this information with your lawyer prior to trial.

Makeup of the Court System

In Alabama, almost all family, divorce and child-related matters are handled by the District and Circuit Courts. Generally, the District Courts hear all juvenile cases or those involving illegitimate children. The Circuit Court judges usually hear divorce cases.

Judges hear virtually all cases involving divorce and post-divorce modifications. In the major cities of our state, certain courts are designated to hear only family issues involving juveniles. In Jefferson County, for instance, there are three judges who only hear divorce cases in the Circuit Court. Two judges hear all family court matters that involve juveniles and illegitimate children in the district courts. The system works differently when you live outside the major cities. Circuit Court judges in the smaller counties hear a variety of cases, from divorce to criminal cases to other civil suits. There are advantages to both kinds of judges, but it is critically important to know what kind of judge you have in your case.

Before attending a trial, it is important for you and your lawyer to review the relevant facts in your case. Each hearing will affect your case, and you and your lawyer should be in direct communication concerning the preparation of your case. Prior to any hearing, your lawyer will likely request that you schedule an appointment to prepare for the hearing. The lawyer should take you through the steps of the hearing and explain to you the relevant issues which will need to be addressed at the hearing.

Preparation for Court

In complicated cases that warrant extensive witness preparation, your lawyer may prepare you for the hearing by asking you questions similar to those he will ask you at trial. In addition, he should also prepare you for the multitude of questions the opposing lawyer will ask. If your lawyer tells you something that you absolutely must address at the hearing, follow his or her advice. Most divorce experts know exactly what relevant information each judge wants and needs to hear in order to make a decision. If your lawyer advises you not to discuss a certain issue, follow his advice. For example, many people often want the judge to hear each and every detail of their marriage. The lawyer is keenly aware of the judge's limited time and the possibility the judge will become frustrated if he or she is overwhelmed with irrelevant or repetitive details.

The lawyer needs to know all of the facts and details surrounding the marriage, but then you and your lawyer must determine the best manner in which to tell your side of the story. For example, once you have established in court that a spouse has had an adulterous relationship or been abusive to the other spouse, your lawyer must determine how many additional details are required. If the lawyer wastes too much of the judge's time listing the same facts over and over, the judge may turn his anger away from the other party and focus it on the client who is wasting his time. It is much smarter to move on to avoid giving the opposing party an additional opportunity to rehabilitate his or her testimony. As a result, you may not get to tell the judge everything you want to tell him. If it is not in your best interest to tell him something, follow your lawyer's advice.

When you are testifying at trial and the other side asks you questions, you will be limited in your responses. If the other side asks you a "yes or no" question, it should be answered with "yes" or "no." Many clients have a tendency to want to say, "Yes, but that is because he ...." Your lawyer will give you an opportunity to tell your side of the story, but the other side will limit your testimony to those facts that help their side. For example, the other side may say, "Have you ever yelled at your children?" If the answer is yes, most parents will want to explain. Most people become frustrated when the lawyer on the other side cuts them off and says, "No sir, answer the question with yes or no only." In that type of situation, your lawyer will simply give you an opportunity to add to your answer during the time he is questioning you. The fact that your testimony will be limited can be frustrating to most clients. I recommend that you practice this type of questioning with your lawyer prior to trial, to become familiar with the necessary responses. Generally, this type of practice session will help you because you will know your lawyer is going to cover the necessary points during the presentation of your case, regardless of the manner in which the other side badgers you during the trial.

What the Judge Needs to Know

Many clients believe they need to tell the judge everything about their spouse that is distasteful. However, the judge does not need to know each and every fight the parties ever had or each and every meal you ever prepared. This does not mean the judge is not interested, but the judge needs to hear only the heart of the case. Judges often say they have heard enough on a particular issue and it is time to move on. Failing to heed the judge's advice can result in an unfavorable ruling because you have not heeded his advice. Even if you do not like the advice, keep in mind that the judge will determine the fate of your case. We tell clients that arguing with the judge is similar to arguing with your former junior high principal. If you were called into the principal's office, arguing with the principal would likely result in a more stringent punishment. Likewise, if you argue with the judge, don't be surprised when you get a less-than-favorable result.

Friend: *How'd your divorce*
               trial go?

Spouse: *My lawyer chewed her up.*

Friend: *Well, what all did you get?*

Spouse: *Oh, she got everything, but*
               we sure let her have it!

CHAPTER 23

Your Divorce Trial

Sometimes a client is more concerned about humiliating the witness on the witness stand than in reaching the best possible settlement. Assuming you are unable to settle your case, eventually it will be set for trial on the court's calendar. I say "eventually" because with so many cases on the docket, you might wait as long as two years after the divorce is filed to finalize the divorce. The first case setting usually is three months or more after the filing of the divorce complaint. It is not uncommon for a case to be continued several times before it actually reaches trial. Continuances occur for a variety of reasons: the parties' readiness to try the case, conflicts in the attorneys' schedules, conflicts in the client's schedule and conflicts in the court's docket. If the judge is already in trial on another case, has an immediate issue to address or an older case to hear, your case may be passed over and continued to a later date.

It is a common strategy for some attorneys representing a spouse who will likely have financial obligations to the other spouse after the divorce to continue the case as long as possible. This either avoids imposing a premature obligation on the client or forces a settlement in the case. Over time, many people become anxious to settle the case, even accepting an inadequate settlement offer, due to the length

143

of time they have been involved in a pending divorce. Once a decision has been made that a settlement cannot be reached, it may be a long time before the case actually goes to trial. The delay needs to be factored into any decisions surrounding the settlement of the case and whether the expenses associated with the delay will be outweighed by the trial court's potential ruling.

In my experience, many opposing spouses do not believe the other spouse will follow through with going to trial. This is usually in those cases where the opposing spouse dominated the other spouse throughout the marriage. In this type of situation, it is often beneficial for the spouse to follow through with the trial. Otherwise, the difficult spouse will continue to harass the more congenial one after the divorce, believing he or she can get away with it.

Your Appearance at Court

For any court appearance, clients should dress professionally. For men, I generally recommend a suit or nice pair of slacks, a white shirt and a tie. A "church" dress or suit is appropriate for a female. If you have any questions about your wardrobe choices, be sure to ask your lawyer or his staff for suggestions. First impressions are important in all aspects of life, but perhaps they are most important in a custody or marital dispute where a judge is forced to evaluate the credibility of the parties from a limited viewpoint.

From the moment you leave your house, until you enter the courthouse, act in a mature and professional manner. You never know who might see or hear you. You cannot even imagine the look on a judge's face when he hears about a party threatening the other party in the hallway.

At the hearing, be calm and cool, even though deep down you may be quite the opposite. Many cases have been settled because a client came to court poker faced, convincing the other side they were confident in their position and not concerned about going to trial.

The Court's Docket

The courthouse will be an eye-opening experience for you. Most clients have only seen a courthouse through a television set or on a movie screen. Real life in court is different from life on television. For example, 10 to 15 cases may be set on the judge's docket the same day, along with your case. These cases range from very brief motions to other cases set for trial. The parties and witnesses for each case on the docket fill the courtroom. The hallways outside the courtroom are often lined with hard wood benches filled to capacity with more parties, witnesses and lawyers trying to resolve their cases.

The first thing that usually happens in the morning is for the judge to call his docket. This means the judge briefly calls each case and checks the status with the attorneys representing the parties. This may involve the attorneys requesting an opportunity to determine if a settlement is possible. It can also involve a range of other issues, from requesting a continuance to asking to speak with the judge about a particular issue in the case that needs clarification before the case can proceed. If the parties are ready for trial, the judge will determine, based on all of the cases he has set that day, which case he will hear that day.

The judge's determination is based on a variety of factors. First, the oldest case usually has priority. The filing date of your case determines the age of your case. This means that if your case was filed three months ago and another case was filed 15 months ago, the older case has priority. Also, the judge will look at the seriousness of the issue at hand. For example, if there is an emergency issue on the docket — such as an immediate threat of abuse or theft of property — the court usually attempts to resolve these issues, even if it is only a short-term fix.

However, when there are 10 to 15 "emergencies" set on the court's docket the same day as your case, the judge will pick the "greatest emergency" that time will permit him to handle that day. If the judge is already in trial on a case from the previous day, usually he will keep going on that case and continue all of the others. This is simply the judicial system in action, and seldom can your lawyer do anything about it. What this means to you is that even though you waited three months to get to trial, you prepared for the trial with your lawyer, and your witnesses are all present at the courthouse, your case still may be continued over your lawyer's objections. It is imperative that you recognize in the beginning that your divorce case could be over in a week, but it could also last up to two years or more, regardless of how badly you want to be divorced right now.

If extended travel or other hardships exist that may make it difficult for a party to come to court, your lawyer may be able to call the courthouse on the day before your case is set to determine the likelihood your case will go to trial. Some judges will tell the lawyer that he is in trial or has a more pressing case that must get resolved. This helps the lawyer avoid imposing a inconvenience on his client. If you have out-of-town witnesses, it is helpful if they can avoid a wasted trip to the courthouse. However, certain judges will require you and your lawyer to be at the courthouse every time the case is set. If your lawyer is an expert in this area, he should be able to tell you whether the judge and his office can help coordinate the scheduling of the trial.

How to Present Yourself

During the hearing, remain focused on the issue at hand. Sit up straight in your seat and speak clearly. Likewise, be polite and remember that the judge is evaluating your responses as well as your demeanor and overall personality in attempting to determine whether you are the evil spouse the other party says you are. Do not be argumentative or hostile with the other side, or answer any questions in a haughty fashion. Remember, your lawyer needs to handle the relevant arguments and not you. The talented trial lawyer on the other side will want to get you upset on the stand, so that you will lose your temper and show the judge the evil personality that the other side has talked about. Human nature makes us all want to respond when we are confronted by another person. Keep in mind that the other side's goal is to get you into an argument and affect your focus during the trial. Do not help them achieve their goal.

Answering Questions at Trial

When you are questioned by the other side, give truthful and accurate answers. Besides the fact that lying on the stand is unethical and illegal, it may ruin your credibility in front of the trial judge if the other side can discredit your testimony. If you expect questions about adultery, abuse, or other secrets that led to the breakup of the marriage, you need to discuss with your lawyer ahead of time how to handle these issues at trial. While you need to tell the truth in your testimony, you should not offer more information than has been requested by the other side.

It is not your job to prove the other side's case. If the lawyer does not ask the appropriate questions, you may not have to provide certain information. This principle applies to every question you are asked. Once you have answered the question as briefly as possible, be quiet. If you have concerns about how to answer certain questions, you need to discuss these questions with your lawyer before trial.

Your lawyer will go over a specific plan for handling the case at trial. You need to follow your lawyer's advice and not venture out into new territory during the course of the trial. Your lawyer will prepare the case based on the information he has at hand and how he knows the judge in that particular court will respond to certain information. Even though you may think certain information or evidence is absolutely imperative to "clear your good name," it may also annoy the judge and throw your lawyer off if you venture into new areas. Most divorce lawyers want to know exactly what you plan to say when you are on the stand. Once the testimony has been discussed, you will need to follow the lawyer's advice as to how to address and deal with specific issues. It is foolish for you not to follow your lawyer's advice. Your refusal to follow your lawyer's advice may cause you to lose your case.

The Final Judgment of Divorce

Upon the final resolution of the divorce, the judge will sign a document called a Final Judgment of Divorce. This document divorces the parties and spells out the terms and conditions of the divorce. If the case was settled, the Final Judgment of Divorce will usually adopt the settlement agreement signed by the parties and make it binding on both parties. If the case was tried in court, the Final Judgment will spell out the court's ruling concerning the trial. It is important that you read and understand all of the terms and conditions of the Final Judgment and the settlement agreement, since you can be held in contempt for not abiding by the terms of the agreement. If you have questions or concerns, your lawyer needs to explain all of the terms and conditions of the settlement agreement or Final Judgment, to ensure that you know your rights and responsibilities. Emotions are at a high level during a trial or during the settlement of the case. You need to understand all of the conditions of the divorce. For example, many terms may change several times during the course of working out a settlement. It is normal for people to forget certain issues, such as the exact property distribution from the marital residence. Make certain you understand the final terms. You should also put the Final Judgment in a place for safekeeping, since you will likely refer to it in the future as disputes or questions arise about the divorce.

NOTES:

PART THREE

What Happens After the Divorce

*Appealing a divorce is like
redrilling a root canal.
If it was done right the first time,
why would it be necessary?*

Anonymous

CHAPTER 24

Appealing Your Divorce Decree

As a general rule, in a divorce action you have one bite at the apple. Your appeal options for relief of the trial court's decisions are limited and rare. However, it may be possible to attack the court's ruling provided strict time limits are met. There are several avenues available for post-judgment review and relief.

Motion to Set Aside or for a New Trial

Either party has the right to file a motion to set aside the decree or request a new trial if the party is not satisfied with the court's ruling. Under Alabama law, this type of motion generally must be filed within 30 days of the date of the order being attacked. These motions usually are not successful unless the court failed to consider a material fact in evidence, or if the court made a clear and distinct error in its ruling. Since the trial judge heard the entire trial, he is familiar with the case and can review his notes to determine if an error occurred. If this type of motion is not successful, a party is then forced to use the appeal process to change the decree.

Time Limits for Appeal

Either party has the right to appeal a Final Judgment of Divorce. Under Alabama law, a notice of an appeal must be filed within 42 days after the judgment is entered or from the day the post-trial motion is denied, whichever is later. It is difficult to win on appeal and there is a presumption in favor of the divorce decree by the trial court, which saw and heard the evidence and the witnesses. The Court of Appeals is limited on review to the evidence that was presented at trial. As a result, it is wise to have a court reporter record the testimony and any rulings made during the trial in order to have an exact record on appeal.

An appeal is a last-ditch effort to change the divorce decree, and often an appeal will fail. The law is specific as to what issues can and cannot be appealed, and the standard of review for such an appeal is stringent. Many people are shocked to find that their failure to present crucial evidence at trial may ruin their chances for an appeal.

Lastly, an appeal is an expensive legal procedure that can cost far more than the divorce process itself. The lawyer must write a history of the case for the Court of Appeals, as well as a history of the testimony at trial. If another lawyer handles the appeal, he will have to spend a considerable amount of time getting familiar with the facts of the case before he can write the appeal. If the appeal is not successful and the matter is then appealed to the Supreme Court, the lawyer may have to draft additional documents and the client will incur additional costs. Therefore, it is much more effective to handle the case properly at trial than to rely on the appeal process to remedy an injustice that occurred at trial.

Where force is necessary, one should make use of it boldly, resolutely, and right to the end. But it is as well to know the limitations of force; to know where to blend force with manoeuvre, assault with conciliation.

Lev Trotsky

CHAPTER 25

The Tough Stuff Begins:
Enforcing Your Divorce Decree

Enforcing a court order can be the most trying part of the divorce process, depending on how the parties feel about each other when it's over.

Contempt Actions

The payment of alimony, child support and attorney's fees, certain types of financial and property matters and child custody can be enforced by an action for contempt against the opposing party. The party bringing the contempt action must show that the opposing party has made a willful refusal to comply with a judgment or order of the court. For example, if a party has failed to pay his child support, but has worked during the entire time of the contemptuous behavior and has chosen to spend the money on other things, most likely you can establish a willful refusal.

It's a different case if the opposing party has lost his job through no fault of his own and did not have an income during the time he failed to make child support payments. Resolution of this issue will depend on the circumstances surrounding the failure to comply with the decree and the party's ability to explain the job loss. Likewise, a parent can be held in contempt for failing to comply with a visitation schedule or for not returning the child to the custodial parent.

Remember that under a contempt action, often you are asking the court to put the opposing party in jail for his or her failure to comply with the decree. In many cases, this is necessary to show the offending party that the obligation must be met. But do you really want to put your children's mother or father in jail? Certainly this action is likely to further diminish your relationship. As a result, you must weigh the seriousness of the contempt against the stark reality of jailing your ex-mate. Under a contempt action, a party may be placed in jail for the contempt and released by purging himself of the contempt action. For example, the court may order the opposing party to jail until he or she pays all or most of the back child support. If the party is financially unable to pay, the court may not keep him in jail. The old saying that you can't get blood from a turnip may apply in that situation. Often relatives or new spouses come forward to pay the amount due. It is amazing how quickly a person can come up with money when it means going to jail if they do not pay.

You can often predict compliance problems with your former spouse prior to the final resolution of the case. If this is a possibility in your case, you need to ask your attorney how to limit the possibility of contempt in your divorce. If the party begins acting contemptuously, you need to keep detailed records of payments and obligations that have not been met.

Stand Up to Your Ex

You need to give the opposing party adequate time to comply before filing a contempt action, but it's important not to wait too long to file. Many clients wait until they are owed tens of thousands of dollars before filing an action. Even if they are successful on the contempt action, often they will have to accept installment payments to enable the opposing party to pay off the large debt. Each party should keep detailed records of every support payment received or paid under the divorce decree, to establish a payment history in any future contempt action.

As a final note, a contempt action needs to be filed as soon as is practicable after the party fails to comply, so the payor realizes the payee will not tolerate noncompliance. Your relationship with the opposing party after the divorce will be directly related to your initial actions. If a husband violates the court order without any complaint from the wife, it is likely that the husband will continue this action in the future. If the wife establishes that she will not tolerate missed child support payments or the husband refusing to return the child at a scheduled time, the wife may be able to limit the contemptuous behavior of the husband.

Unfortunately, certain spouses constantly refuse to abide by the decree. This type of spouse should be placed in jail for failure to comply with the decree. While this is an unfortunate situation, it is critical that the offending party be placed in jail to send a message to that spouse, as well as others, that compliance with a court order is necessary and required. When people in the courtroom witness the sheriff taking a party to jail for contempt, great efforts are made to work out problems between the parties.

*Criminal lawyers see the worst
people at their best.
Divorce lawyers see the best
people at their worst.*

Thomas B. Concannon, former divorce lawyer

CHAPTER 26

Seeking Modification
of Your Divorce Decree

A change in circumstances after the original divorce decree was entered may require you to modify certain provisions of the decree. The most common modifications involve custody, child support, visitation and alimony. The law surrounding a Petition to Modify is very limited, and a determination as to whether a modification is possible must be made on a case-by-case basis.

Accordingly, do not rely on a modification down the road if your initial divorce agreement does not work out. Instead, you should obtain the best possible result in the initial divorce agreement and rely on the modification process only to correct an unforeseen change in circumstances.

Custody Modifications

When the parties do not agree after the divorce about the raising of children, one party usually attempts to change the custody arrangement. It is extremely difficult to modify a prior custody award to change custody from one parent to the other. A custody modification is one of the most difficult and expensive forms of post-divorce actions. The positive good brought about by the modification must offset the disruptive effect caused by transferring custody. The court doesn't look at what helps a parent. The judge is sworn to rule in the best interest of the child. A parent seeking to modify custody must show the court that the change would promote the child's best interest and that the child is being adversely affected in the present situation. Often, a party will bring a custody modification when the actual conflict concerns the other spouse and not any impact the spouse has had on the child. It is critical for the party seeking the change to show that the child has actually been affected by the change in circumstances.

Simply because the custodial parent has a new boyfriend or girlfriend, for example, does not mean the child's situation has changed for the worse. If the child has not witnessed any elicit conduct between the parties, the moving party may not be able to establish any actual harm. Just because the non-custodial parent's situation has improved, he will not automatically receive custody in a modification. For example, many mothers who initially gave up custody due to a personal problem mistakenly believe that they will automatically get custody back as soon as they get their lives back together.

This is a mistaken belief, because even though the non-custodial parent's situation has improved, it does not mean there is anything wrong with the way the custodial parent has been caring for the child. If the non-custodial parent can show serious harm to the child, however, it may be possible to modify custody. Keep in mind that harm can be in a variety of forms other than abuse. For example, if the custodial parent is driving while intoxicated, with the child in the car, a reasonable argument can be made that the child's safety is in jeopardy.

Modifying custody is a very difficult area of the law that causes extreme tension and emotion between the parties. Many spouses are upset to find out that they may not be able to change the conditions in which their children are living. Again, this is why it is so important to address all of these concerns under the original divorce decree. It is shocking how many parents give an abusive father either joint custody or substantial visitation rights with a child the father has abused throughout the marriage. It is very difficult to convince a trial judge during a modification proceeding that the father's visitation should be limited, when the mother granted the abusive father expanded visitation, even though she knew that he was abusive.

It may be possible to modify the custody provisions, but you should be ready for a street fight. A custody trial is one of the most difficult and emotionally draining processes you will ever undertake. The legal fees associated with a custody modification can be enormous, and these costs must be weighed in making a decision whether or not to proceed with a modification. If this is an issue in your case, it would be wise to meet with your attorney to determine whether a modification would be in your best interest. Initially, it is best to invest a portion of the potential fees to get your lawyer's opinion on whether you should proceed. If you are not likely to be successful, it is better to know in the beginning

Child Support Modifications

If there is an increase or decrease in the income of either party, it may be possible to modify the prior child support award. If the payor spouse's income has significantly increased, the custodial parent may be due a significant increase in child support. At the same time, if the payor spouse has lost his job or had his income significantly decreased, the payor spouse may be entitled to a reduction in child support. Many parents are due a significant increase in child support because their child support award was calculated prior to the enactment of the Child Support Guidelines in 1989. Many parents are shocked to find out that their child support payment is going up several hundred dollars or more due to changes in the guidelines.

It is also common to modify the child support award to include the payment of college expenses. This modification action must be filed before the child reaches the age of majority (19 in Alabama) or the action will be waived forever. If post-majority college support is an issue, please refer to the earlier section discussing college support under the divorce agreement.

Most divorce experts can calculate the projected new child support payment, provided you have the gross monthly income figures for both parents as well as any day care and health insurance expenses. It is worth noting, however, that a non-custodial parent may attempt to go after custody when the child support modification action is filed. This type of defensive action is usually apparent to the court as an effort to avoid paying higher child support, but it can create considerable problems and expenses for the custodial parent who is seeking an increase in child support. Furthermore, if the custodial parent has had less than exemplary conduct since the divorce, the parent may want to consider not filing a child support modification due to the risk of custody coming into question. For example, if the custodial parent is living with her boyfriend, and this activity is brought to the attention of the trial court by the non-custodial parent, the custodial parent may not only lose on the child support modification, but may also lose custody of the child as well.

Both parents have a duty to support their children. Therefore, if you are aware that the non-custodial parent has had a significant increase in his income, it is very appropriate to request an increase in child support. Your children deserve to enjoy the same lifestyle they would have enjoyed had the parties remained married. However, if the non-custodial parent is paying for a lot of expenses and activities over and above his child support obligation, you may not want to risk all of those extra payments for a slight increase in child support. Obviously, this must be determined based not only on the income of the parties, but also on the facts and circumstances surrounding each particular case. If this is likely to be an issue in your case, you would be wise to sit down with your attorney and discuss the likely new child support payment and the costs associated with achieving such a payment.

Visitation Modifications

After the heat of divorce has cooled, many parents alter visitation between themselves. Informal modifications are common, but they aren't enforceable by law. Most parents find that as their children get older, they and the kids need a little flexibility. This cooperation is recommended, as long as you feel okay about the changes. It is difficult, though, to get such changes mandated by the courts.

Quite often, those changes mean that a non-custodial parent gets more time with the children. For instance, a teenage child may want to take a long trip with that parent, or spend an entire summer with the non-custodial grandparents. Each such request should be carefully considered by the custodial parent, keeping in mind the needs of the child, the ability of the other parent to accept this responsibility, and how the changes may affect your future rights.

The non-custodial parent should not begin to believe that each time he or she makes such a request, the other parent has to go along with it. The other parent still is in charge, and does not have to grant any variations to the agreed-upon visitation schedule.

These modifications, like all others, are very expensive to achieve if you have to go to court. Remember that your children will get older and their circumstances will change. If you and your spouse can remain flexible, you can avoid a lot of heartache down the road.

Alimony Modifications

As stated earlier, certain forms of alimony may be modified in the future. Periodic alimony can be modified if there is change of circumstances in the future. The burden of proving a change is on the party seeking such a change. Both the payor spouse and the recipient spouse can seek a modification of alimony. If the payor spouse's income has decreased significantly, this spouse may be able to request a decrease in the alimony payments. At the same time, if the needs of the recipient spouse have increased, that spouse may be able to request an increase in alimony. Another alimony modification involves requesting an extension of the time period the alimony payments are to be paid.

The law is specific in this area, and the court has held that a party who voluntarily quits his job may not necessarily be awarded a reduction in alimony, depending on the particular circumstances. However, a party who loses his job through no fault of his own, and who suffers a decrease in income, may be entitled to a modification in alimony. When one of the parties relies on the speculation of future events, such as a job change, a petition to modify is likely to be denied as being premature. If a modification is an issue in your case, you would be very wise to meet with your attorney to determine whether a modification is possible in your situation.

Accountant: *I don't recognize the medical procedure noted on this check to your doctor.*
Woman: *The check is to my divorce lawyer. The procedure was a jerkectomy of my ex-husband.*

Randy Nichols,
Divorce Lawyer

CHAPTER 27

The Best Advice:
Do It Right the First Time

Divorce is a mixed bag of complex issues. If you remember anything else from reading these materials, it is that you must attempt to address in the settlement agreement every possible issue you can imagine that may arise post divorce. It is extremely difficult, if not impossible, to modify many provisions after a divorce agreement has been approved by the trial court. Perhaps the best rule of thumb to follow is that if you and your spouse have not been able to agree during the marriage, it is guaranteed that you will not be able to agree on very much after the marriage.

When you are in the midst of a divorce, the last thing you want to consider is getting married again. But the truth is that half of the people who get divorced for the first time will remarry. You should not, however, plan or rely on another marriage. If you leave yourself with intolerable conditions, both financially and in the custody of your children, you may face an unhappy time for years to come.

A young man came to me after his divorce was final. Although the divorce was his wife's idea, he wound up giving her custody of both children and all the marital assets. Also he was paying exorbitant child support and alimony. He did it, he said, "Because I didn't want my kids to suffer." When I questioned the competence of his attorney, the man said, "I gave her all of that, and I didn't think I needed an attorney." Three months after the divorce was final, she moved 2,000 miles away with a man they had both considered a friend, and now he didn't get to see his children (not to mention his furniture) more than once a year. His only relief was the cessation of alimony, since she soon remarried.

The only way to avoid such a tragedy is to consult with an expert familiar in matrimonial law in your area before proceeding with a divorce action. Do not execute any documents without the advice and approval of an attorney. Furthermore, do not rely upon the advice of your spouse's attorney in making a determination of what is an appropriate settlement. Your spouse's attorney cannot advise you as to the consequences of your actions, and his sole purpose is to protect your spouse.

It is likely that your divorce will be one of the most difficult issues you will have to deal with during your lifetime. How you handle the divorce will greatly effect the extent of the problems that you incur after the divorce. Do not believe that your spouse will do "what's right" and nothing will go wrong.

If a divorce is inevitable, you need to arm yourself with a talented divorce lawyer. Consult with your attorney about the actions needed to protect yourself, and get prepared to go into battle. Hopefully, you will avoid going to war. But if you are prepared to do so, you will likely prevent a bad situation from becoming an impossible one.

It's like a new client seeking a modification told me recently: "I had no idea how much of my future would be closely related to the divorce agreement I signed years ago. If only I had been aware of all the issues that would come up and would have hired an expert at that time."

Now she understands what's necessary to obtain THE SUCCESSFUL DIVORCE.

NOTES:

Appendices of Exhibits And Sample Documents

All of the following exhibits are prepared to illustrate various avenues for trial preparation in your case. The people described are not meant to represent anyone living or deceased.

No real names or precise fact patterns have been used to protect the privacy of the parties involved. Any similarity between people or situations is purely coincidental.

Appendix A

CLIENT: _____

ESTIMATED MONTHLY LIVING EXPENSES

	CURRENTLY	POST DIVORCE	RECEIPTS AVAILABLE
FIXED EXPENSES:			
House payment or rent	$	$	
Insurance			
Home	$	$	
Automobile	$	$	
Health	$	$	
Life	$	$	
Other			
Taxes - Home	$	$	
FLEXIBLE EXPENSES:			
Electricity	$	$	
Gas or Oil (Heat)	$	$	
Telephone	$	$	
Water and Sewer	$	$	
Cable Television	$	$	
Pest Control	$	$	
Yard Care	$	$	
Household Help	$	$	
Repair/Maintenance	$	$	
Other	$	$	
FOOD:			
Groceries	$	$	
Restaurants	$	$	
Lunches - You	$	$	

Appendix A

	CURRENTLY	POST DIVORCE	RECEIPTS AVAILABLE
TRANSPORTATION:			
Car Payment	S	S	
Gas and Oil	S	S	
Repairs/Maintenance	S	S	
Auto Tag and Taxes	S	S	
CHILDREN:			
Private School, Tutors, etc.	S	S	
Activities (Sports, Music, Scouts, etc.)	S	S	
School Lunches	S	S	
Other School Costs	S	S	
CLOTHING/PERSONAL:			
Clothes - You	S	S	
Clothes - Children	S	S	
Shoes	S	S	
Accessories	S	S	
Laundry/Dry Cleaning	S	S	
Beauty Shop/Barber	S	S	
Cosmetics	S	S	
ENTERTAINMENT:			
Newspapers, Magazines, Books	S	S	
Sports, Movies, etc.	S	S	
Vacations	S	S	
Other Entertainment	S	S	
EDUCATION:			
Tuition:_____(School)	S	S	
Textbooks, Notebooks, Binders, etc.	S	S	

Appendix A

	CURRENTLY	POST DIVORCE	RECEIPTS AVAILABLE
MISCELLANEOUS COSTS/EXPENSES:			
Religious Contribution	$	$	
Gifts (Birthdays, Holidays, etc.)	$	$	
Taxes Withheld	$	$	
Savings	$	$	
IRA, Other Retirement	$	$	
MEDICAL:			
Doctors	$	$	
Dentists	$	$	
Orthodontist	$	$	
Optometrist	$	$	
Medicine/Prescriptions	$	$	
Other	$	$	
CREDIT CARDS: (Itemize with Balance Due)	Minimum Payment	Minimum Payment	
	$	$	
	$	$	
	$	$	
	$	$	
	$	$	
	$	$	
	$	$	
PERSONAL LOANS: (Please Itemize)			
	$	$	
TOTALS	$	$	
MONTHLY SHORTAGE OR SURPLUS	$		

Appendix B

STATE OF ALABAMA UNIFIED JUDICIAL SYSTEM FORM CS-41	CHILD SUPPORT OBLIGATION INCOME STATEMENT/AFFIDAVIT	CASE NUMBER DR 99 1234

IN THE <u>Circuit</u>   COURT OF <u>Jefferson</u>   COUNTY

<u>Jane Doe</u>   V. <u>John Doe</u>

         PLAINTIFF   DEFENDANT

AFFIDAVIT

I, <u>Jane Doe</u>   , being duly sworn upon my oath, state as follows:

1. I am the [X] plaintiff [ ] defendant in the above entitled matter. My social security number is: 000-00-0000
2. I am [X] currently employed. My employer's name and address is:

                                                  , AL   0

[ ] Not currently employed.
My last employer's name and address is: _____

Last position title _____
Average monthly salary last year of employment: _____

3. My gross monthly income includes:
(For examples of income that must be included, see back of form.)
If income varies by month, enter the estimated average monthly income.)

Employment income	$ 1000.00
Self-employment income	$ 0.00
Other employment-related income	$ 0.00
Other non-employment related income	$ 0.00
Total	$ 1000.00

3a. I incur the following amount monthly $ 250.00
     for child care.   (If none, write None)

3b. The child(ren) of the parties is/are
     [ ] not covered by health insurance
        from me and/or my employer.
     [X] covered by health insurance and I
        pay the following amount monthly
        for the insurance coverage. $ 0.00
                                      (If none, write None)

4. I understand that I will be required to maintain all income documentation used in preparing this affidavit (including my most recent income tax return) and that such documentation shall be made available as directed by the court.

5. I understand that any intentional falsification of the information presented in this income statement/affidavit shall be deemed contempt of court.

                                     Affiant _____

Sworn to and subscribed before me this
   <u>10th</u> day of <u>April</u>   , <u>1997</u>.

Signature _____

Title _____

                    | 8208ADD0 |

Appendix B

```
┌─────────────────────────────────┬──────────────────────────────┬─────────────────────┐
│ STATE OF ALABAMA                │ CHILD SUPPORT OBLIGATION     │ CASE NUMBER         │
│ UNIFIED JUDICIAL SYSTEM         │ INCOME STATEMENT/AFFIDAVIT   │ DR 99 1234          │
│ FORM CS-41                      │                              │                     │
└─────────────────────────────────┴──────────────────────────────┴─────────────────────┘
```

IN THE Circuit _____ COURT OF Jefferson _____ COUNTY

Jane Doe _____ V. John Doe _____
    PLAINTIFF   DEFENDANT

AFFIDAVIT

I, John Doe _____, being duly sworn upon my oath, state
as follows:
1. I am the [ ] plaintiff [X] defendant in the above entitled matter.
 My social security number is: _____ 000-00-0000 _____
2. I am [X] currently employed. My employer's name and address is:
_____
_____, AL 0 _____
   [ ] Not currently employed.
My last employer's name and address is: _____

Last position title _____
Average monthly salary last year of employment: _____
3. My gross monthly income includes:
(For examples of income that must be included, see back of form.
If income varies by month, enter the estimated average monthly income.)
  Employment income $_____2000.00
  Self-employment income $_____0.00
  Other employment-related income $_____0.00
  Other non-employment related income $_____0.00
    Total $_____2000.00
 3a. I incur the following amount monthly $_____0.00
   for child care.   (If none, write None)
 3b. The child(ren) of the parties is/are
  [ ] not covered by health insurance
   from me and/or my employer.
  [X] covered by health insurance and I
   pay the following amount monthly
   for the insurance coverage. $_____164.00
           (If none, write None)
4. I understand that I will be required to maintain all income
documentation used in preparing this affidavit (including my most recent
income tax return) and that such documentation shall be made available as
directed by the court.

5. I understand that any intentional falsification of the information
presented in this income statement/affidavit shall be deemed contempt of
court.

             Affiant _____
Sworn to and subscribed before me this
 10th day of April _____, 1997.

Signature _____

Title _____
         | 8208ADD0 |

Appendix B

STATE OF ALABAMA UNIFIED JUDICIAL SYSTEM FORM CS-42	CHILD SUPPORT GUIDELINE FORM	CASE NUMBER DR 99 1234

IN THE _Circuit_ COURT OF _Jefferson_ COUNTY

Jane Doe V. John Doe
_____Plaintiff_____ _____Defendant_____

CHILDREN	DOB	CHILDREN	DOB
Mark Doe	12/15/87	Mary Doe	03/01/90

	Plaintiff	Defendant	COMBINED
1. MONTHLY GROSS INCOME	$ 1000.00	$ 2000.00	
a. Minus Preexisting Child Spt Pmt	- 0.00	- 0.00	
b. Minus Preexisting Alimony Pmt	- 0.00	- 0.00	
2. MONTHLY ADJUSTED GROSS INCOME	$ 1000.00	$ 2000.00	$ 3000.00
3. PERCENTAGE SHARE OF INCOME (Parent's Income/Combined Income)	33.3%	66.7%	
4. BASIC CHILD SUPPORT OBLIGATION (Apply Line 2 Combined to Child Support Schedule)			$ 677.00
5. Work-Related Child Care Costs			+ 250.00
6. Health Insurance Costs			+ 164.00
7. TOTAL CHILD SUPPORT OBLIGATION (Add lines 4, 5, and 6)			$ 1091.00
8. EACH PARENT'S SUPPORT OBLIGATION (Multiply Line 7 by Line 3)	$ 363.30	$ 727.70	
9. Adjustment for Payment of Health	$ 0.00	$ 164.00	
10. RECOMMENDED CHILD SUPPORT ORDER (Get Line 6 for the non-custodial parent only. Leave custodial blank)	$	$ 563.70	

Comments, Calculations, or Rebuttals to Schedule:

PREPARED BY: John M. Wood DATE: 04/10/97
|8208ADD0|

Appendix B

STATE OF ALABAMA UNIFIED JUDICIAL SYSTEM FORM CS-43	CHILD SUPPORT GUIDELINES NOTICE OF COMPLIANCE	CASE NUMBER DR 99 1234

IN THE <u>Circuit</u>   COURT OF <u>Jefferson</u>   COUNTY

<u>Jane Doe</u>   V. <u>John Doe</u>
      PLAINTIFF   DEFENDANT

[X] Based upon the income and expenditures supplied by the parties in the Form CS-41, Child Support Obligation Income Statement/Affidavit, the Child Support Guidelines, as set out in Rule 32 of the Alabama Rules of Judicial Administration, have been followed and applied.

[ ] The requirements of Rule 32, Child Support Guidelines, Alabama Rules of Judicial Administration, have not been met due to the following:

Date: _____   Date: _____

_____   _____
Signature of Plaintiff   Signature of Defendant

_____   _____
Signature of Plaintiff's Attorney   Signature of Defendant's Attorney

_____   _____
Address of Plaintiff or Attorney   Address of Defendant or Attorney

_____   _____
Phone # of Plaintiff or Attorney   Phone # of Defendant or Attorney

_____   _____

8208ADD0

Appendix B

STATE OF ALABAMA UNIFIED JUDICIAL SYSTEM FORM CS-41	CHILD SUPPORT OBLIGATION INCOME STATEMENT/AFFIDAVIT	CASE NUMBER

IN THE _____ COURT OF _____ COUNTY

_____ v. _____

PLAINTIFF   DEFENDANT

AFFIDAVIT

I, _____, being duly sworn upon my oath, state as follows:

1. I am the [ ] plaintiff [ ] defendant in the above entitled matter. My social security number is: _____

2. I am [ ] currently employed. My employer's name and address is:

_____, AL 0 _____

[ ] Not currently employed.
My last employer's name and address is: _____

Last position title _____
Average monthly salary last year of employment: _____

3. My gross monthly income includes:
(For examples of income that must be included, see back of form. If income varies by month, enter the estimated average monthly income.)

Employment income	$_____
Self-employment income	$_____
Other employment-related income	$_____
Other non-employment related income	$_____
Total	$_____

3a. I incur the following amount monthly for child care. $_____
(If none, write None)

3b. The child(ren) of the parties is/are
[ ] not covered by health insurance from me and/or my employer.
[X] covered by health insurance and I pay the following amount monthly for the insurance coverage. $_____
(If none, write None)

4. I understand that I will be required to maintain all income documentation used in preparing this affidavit (including my most recent income tax return) and that such documentation shall be made available as directed by the court.

5. I understand that any intentional falsification of the information presented in this income statement/affidavit shall be deemed contempt of court.

_____
Affiant

Sworn to and subscribed before me this _____ day of _____, _____.

_____
Signature

_____
Title

8208ADD0

182

Appendix B

STATE OF ALABAMA UNIFIED JUDICIAL SYSTEM FORM CS-42	CHILD SUPPORT GUIDELINE FORM	CASE NUMBER

IN THE _____ COURT OF _____ COUNTY

_____ v. _____
Plaintiff   Defendant

CHILDREN	DOB	CHILDREN	DOB

	Plaintiff	Defendant	COMBINED
1. MONTHLY GROSS INCOME	$	$	
a. Minus Preexisting Child Spt Pmt	-	-	
b. Minus Preexisting Alimony Pmt	-	-	
2. MONTHLY ADJUSTED GROSS INCOME	$	$	$
3. PERCENTAGE SHARE OF INCOME (Parent's Income/Combined Income)	%	%	
4. BASIC CHILD SUPPORT OBLIGATION (Apply Line 2 Combined to Child Support Schedule)			$
5. Work-Related Child Care Costs			+
6. Health Insurance Costs			+
7. TOTAL CHILD SUPPORT OBLIGATION (Add lines 4, 5, and 6)			$
8. EACH PARENT'S SUPPORT OBLIGATION (Multiply Line 7 by Line 3)	$	$	
9. Adjustment for Payment of Health	$	$	
10. RECOMMENDED CHILD SUPPORT ORDER (Get Line 6 for the non-custodial parent only. Leave custodial blank)	$	$	

Comments, Calculations, or Rebuttals to Schedule:

PREPARED BY:	DATE:

|8208ADD0|

183

Appendix B

STATE OF ALABAMA UNIFIED JUDICIAL SYSTEM FORM CS-43	CHILD SUPPORT GUIDELINES NOTICE OF COMPLIANCE	CASE NUMBER

IN THE _____ COURT OF _____ COUNTY

_____ v. _____
       PLAINTIFF   DEFENDANT

[ ] Based upon the income and expenditures supplied by the parties in the Form CS-41, Child Support Obligation Income Statement/Affidavit, the Child Support Guidelines, as set out in Rule 32 of the Alabama Rules of Judicial Administration, have been followed and applied.

[ ] The requirements of Rule 32, Child Support Guidelines, Alabama Rules of Judicial Administration, have not been met due to the following:

Date: _____   Date: _____

_____   _____
Signature of Plaintiff   Signature of Defendant

_____   _____
Signature of Plaintiff's Attorney   Signature of Defendant's Attorney

_____   _____
Address of Plaintiff or Attorney   Address of Defendant or Attorney

_____   _____
Phone # of Plaintiff or Attorney   Phone # of Defendant or Attorney

8208ADD0

184

Appendix B

Schedule of Basic Child Support Obligations
NUMBER OF CHILDREN DUE SUPPORT

GROSS INCOME	ONE CHILD	TWO CHILDREN	THREE CHILDREN	FOUR CHILDREN	FIVE CHILDREN	SIX CHILDREN
			COMBINED			
			Below			
550.00 Monthly Basic Child Support Obligation Established at the Discretion of the Court						
550.00	50	51	51	52	52	53
600.00	82	83	84	85	86	87
650.00	112	113	114	115	116	118
700.00	141	142	144	145	147	148
750.00	151	172	173	175	177	179
800.00	158	201	203	205	208	210
850.00	166	230	233	235	238	240
900.00	173	259	262	265	268	271
950.00	180	279	291	294	298	301
1000.00	187	290	320	324	327	331
1050.00	194	301	350	354	357	361
1100.00	201	312	379	383	387	391
1150.00	208	323	405	413	417	422
1200.00	215	334	418	442	447	452
1250.00	222	345	432	472	477	482
1300.00	229	356	445	502	508	514
1350.00	236	367	459	518	543	549
1400.00	243	378	474	534	577	584
1450.00	251	390	488	550	599	618
1500.00	257	399	500	564	614	648
1550.00	263	409	512	577	629	672
1600.00	269	418	524	590	643	688
1650.00	275	428	536	604	658	704
1700.00	281	437	548	617	672	719
1750.00	287	447	560	631	687	735
1800.00	294	456	571	644	701	750

Appendix B

1850.00	300	466	583	657	716	766
1900.00	306	475	595	671	730	781
1950.00	312	485	607	684	745	797
2000.00	318	495	619	698	760	813
2050.00	325	505	632	712	775	829
2100.00	331	514	644	726	790	846
2150.00	338	524	656	740	806	862
2200.00	344	534	669	754	821	878
2250.00	350	544	681	768	836	894
2300.00	357	554	694	782	852	911
2350.00	363	563	705	795	865	925
2400.00	368	572	716	807	879	940
2450.00	374	580	727	819	893	954
2500.00	380	589	738	832	906	969
2550.00	386	598	749	844	920	983
2600.00	391	607	760	857	933	998
2650.00	397	616	771	869	947	1012
2700.00	403	625	782	882	961	1027
2750.00	409	633	793	894	974	1042
2800.00	414	642	804	907	988	1056
2850.00	420	651	815	919	1002	1071
2900.00	426	660	826	931	1015	1085
2950.00	431	669	837	944	1029	1100
3000.00	437	677	848	956	1042	1114
3050.00	443	686	859	969	1056	1129
3100.00	449	695	870	981	1070	1143
3150.00	454	704	881	994	1083	1158
3200.00	459	712	891	1005	1096	1171
3250.00	464	720	901	1016	1108	1185
3300.00	469	728	911	1028	1121	1198
3350.00	475	736	922	1039	1133	1211
3400.00	480	745	932	1050	1145	1225
3450.00	485	753	942	1062	1158	1238

3500.00	490	761	952	1073	1170	1252
3550.00	495	769	962	1085	1183	1265
3600.00	500	777	972	1096	1195	1278
3650.00	505	785	982	1107	1208	1292
3700.00	511	794	994	1120	1222	1307
3750.00	517	803	1005	1133	1236	1322
3800.00	523	813	1017	1146	1250	1337
3850.00	529	822	1028	1159	1264	1352
3900.00	534	831	1040	1172	1278	1367
3950.00	540	840	1051	1185	1293	1382
4000.00	546	849	1063	1197	1307	1397
4050.00	552	858	1074	1210	1321	1412
4100.00	558	868	1085	1223	1335	1427
4150.00	563	877	1097	1236	1349	1443
4200.00	569	886	1108	1249	1363	1458
4250.00	575	895	1120	1262	1377	1473
4300.00	581	904	1131	1275	1391	1488
4350.00	587	913	1143	1288	1405	1503
4400.00	592	923	1154	1300	1419	1518
4450.00	598	931	1159	1313	1433	1532
4500.00	604	940	1170	1325	1446	1546
4550.00	609	948	1180	1337	1458	1560
4600.00	614	956	1190	1348	1471	1573
4650.00	619	964	1200	1359	1483	1586
4700.00	624	972	1209	1370	1495	1598
4750.00	629	980	1219	1381	1507	1611
4800.00	635	987	1229	1392	1519	1624
4850.00	640	995	1239	1403	1531	1637
4900.00	645	1003	1249	1414	1543	1650
4950.00	650	1011	1258	1425	1555	1663
5000.00	655	1019	1268	1436	1567	1676
5050.00	660	1027	1278	1447	1579	1689
5100.00	665	1035	1288	1458	1591	1701

Appendix B

5150.00	670	1042	1298	1469	1604	1714
5200.00	675	1050	1307	1481	1616	1727
5250.00	681	1058	1317	1492	1628	1740
5300.00	686	1066	1327	1503	1640	1753
5350.00	691	1074	1337	1514	1652	1766
5400.00	696	1082	1346	1525	1664	1779
5450.00	701	1090	1356	1536	1676	1792
5500.00	706	1097	1366	1547	1688	1805
5550.00	711	1105	1376	1558	1700	1817
5600.00	716	1113	1386	1569	1712	1830
5650.00	722	1121	1395	1580	1724	1843
5700.00	727	1129	1405	1591	1737	1856
5750.00	732	1137	1415	1602	1749	1869
5800.00	737	1145	1425	1613	1761	1882
5850.00	742	1152	1435	1624	1773	1895
5900.00	747	1160	1444	1636	1785	1908
5950.00	752	1168	1454	1647	1797	1920
6000.00	757	1176	1464	1658	1809	1933
6050.00	762	1184	1474	1669	1821	1946
6100.00	768	1192	1483	1680	1833	1959
6150.00	772	1198	1497	1689	1843	1969
6200.00	775	1203	1504	1697	1851	1979
6250.00	779	1209	1511	1705	1860	1988
6300.00	783	1214	1518	1713	1869	1997
6350.00	787	1220	1526	1721	1878	2007
6400.00	790	1226	1533	1729	1886	2016
6450.00	794	1231	1540	1737	1895	2025
6500.00	798	1237	1547	1745	1904	2035
6550.00	802	1243	1554	1753	1913	2044
6600.00	805	1248	1561	1761	1922	2053
6650.00	809	1254	1568	1769	1930	2063
6700.00	813	1259	1575	1777	1939	2072
6750.00	817	1265	1582	1785	1948	2081
6800.00	820	1271	1589	1793	1957	2091

Appendix B

6850.00	824	1276	1597	1801	1965	2100
6900.00	828	1282	1604	1809	1974	2110
6950.00	831	1287	1611	1817	1983	2119
7000.00	835	1293	1618	1825	1992	2128
7050.00	839	1299	1625	1833	2000	2138
7100.00	843	1304	1632	1841	2009	2147
7150.00	846	1310	1639	1849	2018	2156
7200.00	850	1315	1646	1857	2027	2166
7250.00	854	1321	1653	1865	2035	2175
7300.00	857	1326	1660	1872	2043	2183
7350.00	860	1331	1666	1878	2050	2191
7400.00	862	1336	1672	1885	2057	2199
7450.00	865	1340	1678	1891	2064	2207
7500.00	868	1345	1684	1898	2072	2214
7550.00	871	1350	1690	1904	2079	2222
7600.00	874	1355	1696	1911	2086	2230
7650.00	877	1359	1702	1917	2093	2238
7700.00	879	1364	1708	1924	2100	2246
7750.00	882	1369	1714	1930	2107	2254
7800.00	885	1374	1720	1937	2114	2261
7850.00	888	1378	1726	1943	2122	2269
7900.00	891	1383	1732	1950	2129	2277
7950.00	894	1388	1738	1956	2136	2285
8000.00	896	1393	1744	1962	2143	2293
8050.00	899	1397	1750	1969	2150	2300
8100.00	902	1402	1756	1975	2157	2308
8150.00	905	1407	1762	1982	2164	2316
8200.00	908	1412	1768	1988	2171	2324
8250.00	911	1417	1774	1995	2179	2332
8300.00	914	1421	1780	2001	2186	2340
8350.00	916	1426	1785	2008	2193	2347
8400.00	919	1431	1792	2014	2200	2355
8450.00	922	1434	1797	2020	2206	2361

Appendix B

8500.00	924	1438	1801	2025	2212	2367
8550.00	926	1441	1806	2030	2217	2373
8600.00	929	1445	1810	2035	2222	2379
8650.00	931	1448	1815	2040	2228	2384
8700.00	933	1452	1819	2045	2233	2390
8750.00	935	1455	1823	2050	2239	2396
8800.00	938	1459	1828	2055	2244	2401
8850.00	940	1462	1832	2060	2249	2407
8900.00	942	1466	1837	2065	2255	2413
8950.00	945	1469	1841	2070	2260	2418
9000.00	947	1473	1846	2075	2266	2424
9050.00	949	1476	1850	2080	2271	2430
9100.00	951	1480	1854	2085	2276	2435
9150.00	954	1483	1859	2090	2282	2441
9200.00	956	1487	1863	2095	2287	2447
9250.00	958	1490	1868	2100	2293	2453
9300.00	961	1494	1872	2105	2298	2458
9350.00	963	1497	1876	2110	2303	2464
9400.00	965	1501	1881	2115	2309	2470
9450.00	967	1504	1885	2120	2314	2475
9500.00	970	1507	1890	2125	2320	2481
9550.00	972	1511	1894	2130	2325	2487
9600.00	974	1514	1898	2135	2330	2492
9650.00	977	1518	1903	2140	2336	2498
9700.00	979	1521	1907	2145	2341	2504
9750.00	981	1525	1912	2150	2347	2510
9800.00	983	1528	1916	2155	2352	2515
9850.00	986	1532	1921	2160	2357	2521
9900.00	988	1535	1925	2165	2363	2527
9950.00	990	1539	1929	2170	2363	2532
10000.00	992	1542	1934	2175	2374	2538

Appendix C

_____ v. _____

CONFIDENTIAL AND PRIVILEGED

ASSETS	CURRENT VALUE	DEBT	EQUITY	TITLE JOINT	DATE OF PURCHASE
Certificate of Deposit	$10,000.00	-0-	$10,000.00	Joint	06/15/94

Appendix C

_____ v. _____

CONFIDENTIAL AND PRIVILEGED

Name On Debt	Current Balance	Account Number	Monthly Payment	Joint or Individual	Purpose of Debt
John Doe	$4500.00	ABC-1234	$125.00	Individual	Family Items

WOOD & SHAW, L.L.C.
SKELETONS IN THE CLOSET AND SENSITIVE TOPICS

Client (Y or N) Spouse (Y or N)_____

1.   Have you or your (ex) spouse ever committed a felony?_____
2.   Have you or your (ex) spouse ever been in jail?_____
3.   Have you or your (ex) spouse ever used illegal drugs?_____
4.   Have you or your (ex) spouse ever abused prescription
       drugs?_____
5.   Have you or your (ex) spouse ever abused alcohol?_____
6.   Have you or your (ex) spouse ever been arrested or convicted
       of driving while under the influence of alcohol
       (drunk driving)?_____
7.   Have you or your (ex) spouse ever engaged in gambling activities
       (legal or illegal)?_____
8.   Have you or your (ex) spouse ever attempted suicide?_____
9.   Have you or your (ex) spouse ever been hospitalized for an
       emotional or psychiatric condition?_____
10.   Have you or your (ex) spouse ever suffered from or received
       treatment for an emotional psychiatric condition?_____
11.   Have you or your (ex) spouse ever abused your child?_____
12.   Have you or your (ex) spouse ever abused your spouse?_____
13.   Have you or your (ex) spouse ever had a sexual relationship during
       the marriage with someone other than your spouse?_____
14.   Have you or your (ex) spouse ever had a sexual relationship with
       someone other than your spouse of which the minor children were
       aware?_____
15.   Have you or your (ex) spouse ever had a homosexual
       relationship?_____
16.   Have you or your (ex) spouse ever engaged in unusual sexual
       practices?_____
17.   Have you or your (ex) spouse ever had a pregnancy outside of the
       marriage?_____

Date:_____

Client's Signature _____

Appendix D

WOOD & SHAW, L.L.C.
<u>INFORMATION TO BE PROVIDED BY CLIENT</u>

( ) Current wage statement for client and spouse
( ) Federal & State income tax returns for preceding _____ years
( ) Deed(s) to real property
( ) Title and registration document(s) to vehicles, boats and trailers
( ) Details on family insurance program
( ) Narratives:
       ( )   Husband and Wife Fault
       ( )   Childcare Roles
       ( )   Timeline of the Marriage
( ) Estimated monthly living expenses
( ) Details on pension plan (Keogh, IRA, profit sharing, etc.)
( ) Detailed list of personal property with your opinion of the fair market value
( ) Detailed list of family debts
( ) Financial statements furnished to banks or financial institutions
( ) Other:

_____

( ) Other:

_____

( ) Prior pleadings, court orders, decrees
( ) Division of furniture and funishings

Appendix D

This memorandum is an example of the information Wood & Shaw attorneys compile after an initial interview with a client to keep track of the relevant issues in a complicated case.

Memorandum *
Client Notes

CLIENT: Constance W. Seminar ("Connie")
MATTER: Divorce
DATE:
RE: Initial Meeting with Client

CONFIDENTIAL AND PRIVILEGED

I.   CLIENT
        Name: Constance W. Seminar ("Connie")
        Address: 543 Wallingford Estates
                    Birmingham, Alabama 36604
        Telephone Numbers: 555-1234
        Employment: Housewife
                  Wife worked for 2 years as a public school teacher right after the couple got married. She has not worked since 1980.
        Gross monthly income: N/A
        Health insurance costs: N/A

---

* The "Seminar v. Seminar" basic fact pattern is the creation of Randy Nichols, a family law practitioner in Birmingham, Alabama. It has been used in a number of continuing legal educaiton seminars and is adapted for use here with the permission of Mr. Nichols.

Appendix D

II.   OPPOSING PARTY

        Name: Joseph H. Seminar, Jr. ("Joe")

        Address: 123 Main Street, Apartment 456
                        Birmingham, Alabama 36601

        Telephone Numbers: 555-6666 home
                              555-7777 work

        Employment: Seminar & Smith, P.C.
                        5000 University Blvd.
                        Birmingham, Alabama 36651

             Gross monthly income: $8,750.00
             $105,000 1996 W-2 income

             Health insurance costs: unknown

III.   MARITAL HISTORY

             Marriage Date: June 15, 1978
             Marriage Location: Birmingham, Alabama
             Date of Separation: April 25, 1994
             Jurisdiction: Jefferson County

IV.   CHILDREN

Name	Birthdate
Joseph H. Seminar, III, age 12	1/1/82
Mary Constance Seminar, age 10	2/2/84
William Robert Seminar, age 8	3/3/86

             Custody to whom? Wife. Children are presently
                   in the physical custody of the Wife.

V.   CHILD SUPPORT

             Day care expense - unknown. Paid by Husband
             Insurance expense - unknown. Paid by Husband

VI.   FAULT - SEE BACKGROUND

Incompatibility	Him	X	Her	X
Adultery	Him		Her	X
Physical Abuse	Him		Her	
Mental Abuse	Him	X	Her	

VII.   ASSETS

Appendix D

HOUSE:

    The parties jointly own a house located at 543 Wallingford Estates, Birmingham, Alabama. The home was purchased, in part, with funds from the Wife's family. The Wife's family contributed $30,000.00 to the purchase in 1986. This money was termed a "loan" but no written documentation or terms of repayment were obtained from Husband and Wife. The $30,000.00, plus $20,000.00 from the parties original residence provided a $50,000.00 down payment on the present residence.

    The parties agree the residence is worth approximately $240,000.00. There is an outstanding mortgage on the residence of $120,000.00. The monthly payments are $1,075.00. There is a home equity loan from the house for $20,000.00. The Husband used $10,000.00 of the home equity loan to purchase computers for Husband's law firm.

AUTOMOBILES:

Wife:	1993 Acura Legend, paid for
Husband:	1989 Jeep Cherokee, leased to him through his law practice
	1965 Mustang, bought by Husband in 1985. The car is in mint condition and valued at $18,000.00.

FURNITURE AND FURNISHINGS:

    Wife: The Wife values the furniture and furnishings in the home at approximately $25,000.00.

    Husband: The Husband values the furniture and furnishings in the home at approximately $50,000.00.

RETIREMENT AND INVESTMENT ACCOUNTS:

    Husband's IRA - $44,000.00

    Wife's spousal IRA - $6,000.00

Joint Investment Portfolio with Shearson Lehman - $80,000.00 - acquired solely from savings in the last ten years of marriage, invested in a variety of stocks, bonds and mutual funds.

Wife's Investment Portfolio - $53,000.00 - acquired solely from a series of gifts from her family over the course of the marriage.

Husband's Profit Sharing Plan - vested interest of $24,500.00

CHECKING AND SAVINGS ACCOUNTS:

Joint Checking Account with First Alabama Bank - $2,500.00
Joint Money Market Account with SouthTrust Bank - $7,000.00

OTHER ASSETS:

Stock in the Husband's law practice - worth ____??
Wife's fur and jewelry worth approximately $24,000.00
Husband's coin collection worth approximately $6,000.00

VIII.   DEBTS

Mortgage - See discussion on house above.

Credit Cards - The parties owe approximately $4,000.00 for credit cards. We need to verify whether the credit cards are listed jointly or individualiy.

First Alabama Bank - The parties owe approximately $6,000.00 for a loan from the prior year's taxes.

IX.   BACKGROUND

The parties met while the Husband was in law school in Tuscaloosa and the Wife was attending college in Birmingham. The parties married after the Wife's college graduation. The parties have been married for 16 years and have three children. The parties separated on April 25, 1994.

CHILDREN

Wife's Involvement

The children seem to be well adjusted to the current situation and are doing well in school. The Wife stated the children only have a superficial relationship with the Husband and the Wife has been the primary daily caretaker for the children during the marriage. The Wife has bought the children's clothes, arranged their meals, helped with their homework, attended school events, and promoted their religious training.

Husband's Involvement

The Wife stated the Husband has participated very little with the activities and schooling of the children. The Husband has occasionally attended school events and periodically participates in activities with the children.

WIFE'S EMPLOYMENT

The Wife worked for two years as a public school teacher, and elected to leave her career with encouragement from Husband to raise the children.

HUSBAND'S EMPLOYMENT

The Husband worked with a large law firm for two years after law school, and then opened his own law practice. The Husband is a 50% stockholder in Seminar & Smith, P.C., a practice organized in 1980, and he specializes in divorce and family law. Last year, the firm grossed $480,000.00, and the Husband had a 1993 W-2 income of $105,000.00. The firm pays health insurance, life insurance, and disability insurance, and the Husband has a corporate profit sharing plan, with a vested interest of $24,500.00.

Appendix D

BREAKDOWN OF THE MARRIAGE

The Wife has become increasingly bored with the relationship. The Wife has complained to the Husband that he is more devoted to his career than to his family. During the last three years, the Wife has become withdrawn and aloof, and the parties' sexual relationship has suffered. The Wife has complained to the Husband about his lack of affection toward her and lack of any interest in improving the relationship. The Husband apparently believes that he must work all of the time to pay for what he considers to be a standard of living which is "too high for their income."

HUSBAND'S FAULT

Drug Abuse by Husband

During a six month period during law school, Husband abused amphetamines. The abuse was in connection with studying, etc., and he was treated and released after a ten day detox over a school vacation. There has been no relapse, the Husband's father paid for the treatment, and the matter was kept very quiet. Public knowledge of this could cause professional problems. The Husband has continued therapy since his release through a church counselor, who is not a licensed psychiatrist or psychologist.

WIFE'S FAULT

Affair (?)

Summer before last, the Wife took up golf lessons, and was instantly attracted to the golf pro. The wife stated she began having a sexual relationship beginning in December of 1993 with the golf pro. The Wife believes the Husband became suspicious of the affair in April, 1994. The Wife has a concern the Husband hired a private investigator concerning the affair. The Wife has apparently seen someone following her, and has a concern that the investigator may have observed the Wife with the golf pro on several occasions. The Wife is unsure what evidence the investigator may have. **NOTE: Make sure and address any video tapes and/or photographs and/or evidence obtained by the investigator in the interrogatories and requests**

Appendix D

for production.

CONFRONTATION BY HUSBAND REGARDING THE AFFAIR

The Husband confronted the Wife about the affair several weeks ago. The Wife denied the affair. The Husband moved out of the residence after several days.

DIVORCE PLEADINGS FILED BY HUSBAND

The Husband filed a complaint on April 29, 1994 and the Wife was served three days later. No specific allegations of adultery were made in the complaint, and no requests for custody are addressed. The complaint asks for an appropriate order concerning custody, equitable distribution of property, and other relief to which he is entitled.

WIFE'S CONCERN REGARDING THE FACT HUSBAND IS AN ATTORNEY

The Wife stated she was concerned that the lawyer she hired not have a problem handling a case against another domestic lawyer. Apparently, the Husband has been practicing domestic law for some time in this community, and has a positive relationship with the other members of the bar and with the judges. In fact, the Husband apparently goes snow skiing in Switzerland with several of the local attorneys at what the Wife called an "all fun and no work seminar like those held at the Perdido Hilton." Mr. Wood informed the client that he was aware of the political nature of the case.

X.   FEE STRUCTURE

Retainer: The Wife paid an initial retainer of $5,000.00. The Wife was advised by Mr. Wood that fees in this case would be directly related to the time involved in resolving this matter. The Wife had a concern as to an estimate concerning the fees and Mr. Wood informed her that if this matter involved a litigated custody trial, her fees would be considerable. The Wife further stated that she was concerned about the fees, but had family support to help her in this matter.

XI. ISSUES

Is Pendente Lite necessary?	Yes
Possession of homestead?	Yes
Temporary Restraining Order?	Not at this time
Child Support?	Yes
Alimony?	Yes

XI. SETTLEMENT OPTIONS

The Wife was extremely upset during the initial meeting. Mr. Wood advised the Wife to make a list of her present monthly expenses and a list of expenses anticipated in the future in order to determine the Wife's future needs. There was no discussion of any settlement needs during the initial meeting. The Wife scheduled an appointment for the following week to begin working out a settlement proposal with Mr. Wood.

XII. DOCUMENTS TO DRAFT

We need to file an Answer and Counter-Claim immediately requesting alimony, child support, custody and an equitable division of the property. We also need to draft Interrogatories, Requests for Production and Requests for Admissions, and a Motion for Pendente Lite Relief.

Appendix E

Standard Visitation Schedule
For Children Over Three Years Of Age

The standard visitation schedule for children over three years old in many divorces cases generally consists of the following:
- The first and third weekends of each month from 6 p.m. on Friday until 6 p.m. the following Sunday. The first weekend shall begin on the first Friday of each month at 6 p.m.;
- Each Christmas Day from 3 p.m. until 3 p.m. on the following New Year's Day;
- Thirty-one days during the summer (to be taken between June 10 and August 15) to be selected by the non-custodial parent, but upon written notice to the custodial parent at least 30 days in advance of such visitation;
- During the odd years, spring break vacation from 9 a.m. Saturday until the following Friday at 6 p.m.;
- During the even years, Thanksgiving vacation from Wednesday at 6 p.m. until Sunday at 6 p.m.;
- Every other birthday of the child from 6 p.m. on said date until 8 a.m. the following morning;
- Every Father/Mother's Day from 9 a.m. until 6 p.m. of the same day;
- On the birthday of the mother/father from 3 p.m. on said date until 8 p.m. of the same day;
- Any other reasonable times and places upon which the parties can agree; and
- Each party shall keep the other informed on a current basis as to the primary residence, address and telephone number where the children reside or visit.

Standard Visitation Schedule
For Children One To Three Years Of Age

For children over the age of twelve months and under the age of three years, the non-custodial parent shall have the following minimum rights of visitation with any child of the parties as follows:
- On the first and third Sunday of each month from 8 a.m. until 6 p.m.;
- On the birthday of the said child from 6 p.m. until 8 p.m.;

• On each Christmas Day from 10 a.m. until 6 p.m.;

• At all other times mutually agreed upon by and between the husband and wife.

Standard Visitation Schedule
For Children Less Than Twelve Months Of Age

The non-custodial parent shall have the right of visitation with any child under the age of twelve months on the first and third Sunday of each month at the place where the child lives. The periods of visitation are usually limited to three hours in duration or at any other times the parties can agree.

Standard Out Of State Visitation Schedule

If the non-custodial parent lives out of state, the parties may select or be awarded out-of-state visitation due to the difficulty following standard visitation schedules. The out-of-state schedule is primarily tailored to those situations where long distance and airline travel is required. In that event, the standard out-of-state visitation is generally as follows:

• Six weeks during each summer, at a time to be selected by the non-custodial parent, during the child's summer vacation; provided, however that he or she shall have mailed by registered mail a written notice to the custodial parent of the dates of his intended visitation at least thirty days prior to such visitation;

• One week each Christmas holiday, beginning December 26;

• Four days of each spring school holiday;

• Any other reasonable times the non-custodial parent is in the town in which the child resides; and

• Any other times that the parties can agree;

• During any periods of visitation, the said child may travel by commercial airliner provided:

• The non-custodial parent pays all airfare for the transportation of the child.

• The flights are either nonstop or direct and no change of planes is involved until the child reaches the age of fourteen.

Appendix E

- All travel arrangements are made by the non-custodial parent.
- The non-custodial parent notifies the custodial parent not less than ten days before the date of the visitation, of the date, time, airline and flight number of the proposed carrier.
- The non-custodial parent sends the custodial parent the round trip airline tickets and flight number of the proposed carrier, or ensures that they will be at the air terminal.
- The custodial parent delivers the child to the nearest commercial airport offering direct flight service to the airport where the non-custodial parent will receive the child, not to be in excess of 150 miles from his or her residence. The custodial parent shall also pick up the said child at the end of visitation.
- The non-custodial parent ensures that either he or she or the child will notify the custodial parent of the arrival of the child as soon as possible after he or she meets the child.
- Twenty-four hours prior to the time of departure, the non-custodial parent notifies the custodial parent of the dates, times, carrier and flight number of the child's return.
- On return of the child, the custodial parent or the child notify the non-custodial parent of the child's return.

NOTES:

NOTES:

NOTES:

NOTES:

Printed in the United States
3984

9 780965 927307